HOPE IN A SEASON OF SUFFERING

By
Roxanne Eilers

Dedication

This book is dedicated to all those beloved people who are in a season of suffering or have experienced great suffering of many kinds. May God Almighty, in the Name of Jesus, strengthen, establish, settle, and comfort you. Amen.

TABLE OF CONTENTS

HOPE
IN A SEASON OF SUFFERING

Foreword

Have you ever experienced standing on the edge of discouragement, ready to give in to a vast ocean of despair? When difficulties overwhelm you, brokenness and pain can pour in like continuous waves, and hope seems to be lost in an unreachable chasm.

Roxanne Eilers, in her book, *Hope in a Season of Suffering*, offers the kind of help that serves as a life preserver during a flood that threatens to sweep away your soul. She shares her real and authentic story of a season of suffering and how she has been able to emerge triumphant. And here's what you need to know - she has not just barely made it, but is experiencing victorious Christian living, moment by moment. Whether you are seasoned in your spiritual life with Christ, or new in the faith, in her book, you will find practical help for your hurting heart.

Every person experiences those life difficulties that shake the soul. I'll never forget the day I received the news that my mother had fallen and broken her neck. Thus, began a year of life in hospitals, rehabilitation centers, and assisted living care homes. Oh, how I desperately needed a word of encouragement to bring hope in my most difficult hours. You will discover, in the chapters of *Hope in a Season of Suffering,* many words of encouragement to help in your most challenging troubles. Whether you are plagued with fear and worry, experiencing a financial loss, or mourning the death of a loved one, you will find practical principles to bring about a life transformation.

William Ellery has said *in the best books, great men talk to us, give us their most precious thoughts, and pour their souls into ours.* That is exactly what Roxanne has done in *Hope in a Season of Suffering*.

She begins with her story. You will trust from how she tells it that she has lived it. And, I have been privileged to serve together with her in ministry, so I am a firsthand witness as she continues to live it well through the strength of Christ. Following her powerful story, she shares some of the most important principles from God's Word to help anyone who is struggling in their own season of suffering. An added bonus is discussion questions and a Bible study for those who desire to dig deeper. This is a book for all people. It will encourage one in a time of tribulation or offer help to another in trouble.

So, just when you might think everything is over, know that it's always too soon to give up, and the answer may just be around the corner. Grab Roxanne Eilers' book, *Hope in a Season of Suffering*, and get ready to move from discouragement and despair to help and hope.

Catherine Martin

Author and Speaker
Founder, Quiet Time Ministries

Acknowledgments

First, I would like to thank my family. I am grateful for my sister, who journeyed with me through this book from its beginnings. And because this book helped her through a very difficult season in her own life, I am encouraged to share my story with a larger audience. I feel so honored that she believes in me and my work. Then, I want to thank my husband, Ike, who supports me with all his heart and soul and is my faithful companion, whom I love dearly. Thank you to my son, Joseph, for his precious life and belief in me, which has encouraged me to grow—I love him so much. Much thanks to my mother, Jeane, for her undying support, encouragement, inspiration, admiration, and faith in me.

I would also like to thank Barbara Baumann LesStrang for helping to edit this work; she has been a blessing and inspiration in my life. Thank you to Catherine Martin for her encouraging words in the foreword of this book. She is such a special woman of God. Thank you to Marylou Bell for her tremendous help with editing, and her faithful spirit to the Lord Jesus. And, thank you to Susan Campion who performed the final edit on this work and polished it up for publication.

Thank you to all those people who have listened to my stories and given me renewed hope. Thank you to my therapist who was constantly there for me, nursing me back to emotional health, and to my psychiatrist for her wisdom and for being so patient and gentle with me.

Finally, most of all, thank you, thank you to my Savior and Lord, Jesus Christ, who has held me together in my difficult moments, who comforts me, and who will always be my hope! Praise Him forever!

Introduction

Hope in a Season of Suffering is a book for the ordinary person, for the person who is struggling or suffering, for the overwhelmed mother with children, for the man stressed at work, for the daughter or son who need answers, for the grieving person, for the person who is at the end of his or her rope—for the person who needs hope. This book is for you.

In *Hope in a Season of Suffering* you will learn seven basic steps on how to hold on to hope. This book will strengthen your faith and give you support when you need it. The concepts in this book are ones that you will use all of your life.

To begin, it is a good idea to have a notebook for journaling. You could use it for the discussion questions and the Bible studies at the end of each chapter, and then to keep track of your own personal growth and the amazing moments of hope you experience.

I pray this book will be a handbook for you in your times of suffering. Refer to it often as you keep holding on to hope.

Blessings, Roxanne Eilers

The Plans of the Lord stand firm forever; the purposes of His heart through all generations (Psalm 33:11).

Prologue

My mouth went dry, my body shook uncontrollably--I could hardly believe what was happening. I thought I was in a place of no return.

At the age of seventeen, I was convinced my youth had been stolen, snatched away without my consent. And, I was left shattered with an agonizing emotional pain—a pain that no adolescent should ever have to experience.

I felt like a huge, unrelenting tidal wave had struck my life, turning me upside down, spinning it around, and swirling me into the depths of darkness.

But, just before I ran out of air, someone caught my arms and I began to ascend, up, up until my head broke through the surface of the water and I frantically gasped for breath. In the distance, I heard His still small voice calling out to me, "Hold on. I am with you. Hold on to hope."

And so, I did.

Prologue by Barbara LesStrang Baumann

Chapter 1
The Trauma

Winter, 1971, in beautiful Palm Springs, California. I was in my senior year at Palm Springs High School. I was not going to be able to graduate with my friends and classmates because I had missed so many classes. This depressed me along with many other things going on in my life. Coming from a large family and being one of the oldest, I had to care for my four younger siblings, cook, clean, and worry about my studies, and what I was going to do with my future. The latter was a big worry because I had no direction about where I was going or what I wanted to do. I was afraid to grow up and be on my own, and the tradition in our family was to move out when we turned eighteen. I was seventeen and the time was flying by me. It terrified me to think about my future because the world did not seem like a safe place for me, with nuclear weapons that could wipe mankind off the planet, the Vietnam War, protests, and drugs (which I was experimenting with, along with alcohol). Many of my friends were abusing drugs and tripping out on LSD; I had lost some friends through over-doses.

My life was one of bewilderment, fearfulness, confusion and feeling lost. I was continually groping for something to hold on to--something that could make me feel safe; I wanted to be where I felt safe from the problems of the world, my family's problems, and my own personal struggles, which plagued me every day. Just who was I anyway? What was my purpose for living? Why were there so many questions that had no answers? Why was I here?

Then I became obsessed with the fear of death; where would I go when I died? When I was a child and into my early teenage years, having been raised Roman Catholic, I believed that God existed; I often thought about Him. I even prayed to God at night or when I needed help. As I grew older, I bargained with God. I promised Him I wouldn't do bad things and would turn over a new leaf and do what was right--if He helped me out of a jam. God would help me out of my jam, but, of course, I would fail time and time again to keep my part of the bargain. When I went to confession I would confess the same sins over and over; I knew that I was not going to make it to heaven the way I was going. I knew if there was a hell I surely would deserve to go there because of the lifestyle I was choosing. I soon began to question if God really did exist.

Death terrified me day and night--I had to know. Was there a God? If there was, why wouldn't He help me with my problems? I felt so alone and unloved. Where was God in my senior year when I needed Him to take away my fears and show me He was really there?

One night, when I was at the park with one of my friends, we were talking about whether God existed or not. We talked about life on earth and life after death. My friend told me he believed there was no God and that when we die we were as "dead as a dog". This disturbed me very much because I would look up at the yellow moon and the stars at night and think there must be a God. How could we have such a beautiful creation all around us? How could we have emotions of love and hate, happiness and sadness? That night, I left my friend and went home with many questions gnawing at me; I had so many mixed feelings.

As the days went by, I grew more introverted, lost in my own thoughts about living and dying. I could not even concentrate in school, and my grades were dropping lower and lower as I ditched classes to get drunk. Maybe I thought this was a way to forget my fears and worries.

Then something happened in my life that would forever change me--there was no going back. I can't remember what day it was, or what happened at school--all I know is that night I was all alone in my bedroom and I was nervously pacing the floor, feeling like a caged bird. Again, the fears took control of my thoughts and all I could think about was how scary the world seemed. I had no purpose -- there was nowhere to hide.

Suddenly, panic began to grip my body; it shot up my legs, stomach, arms, and neck--I cried out for God to help me--was He there? I continued to feel the horrific panic whelming up within me like a giant tidal wave ready to swallow me and drown me. It seemed like the room began to spin--desperation grabbed me. Then, as my thoughts were madly racing through my mind, something happened.

It was as if a bolt of electricity struck the back of my neck. I stopped and stood, doubled over with emotional pain--then as quick as an electric shock, my brain short-circuited and I found that my mind had shifted from being in reality to being cornered somewhere in unreality. I was hiding somewhere inside myself—at that moment I had clearly lost touch with what was real and had created for myself a world of my own filled with fear instead of security. I know this seems hard to understand, and it is hard to describe, even now over forty years later. My thoughts were zigzagging and became jumbled, and terror gripped me. After a while, the panic began to recede; however, I was shaking uncontrollably and breathing was difficult. What had happened to me?

It wasn't until many years later I learned that I had experienced a severe emotional, mental breakdown. After that I was never the same. My life was changed. I had countless days of emotional and mental suffering waiting in the future . . . beginning the next day.

The next morning, I got up to go to school. I don't know how I even slept the night before; it was probably from exhaustion. That next morning, I was different. My mind, my thoughts, had been shocked into patterns of thinking that I couldn't control-- I had lost touch with reality. I could interact and act like I was normal, but I felt disconnected from the world; things were not normal. I noticed that my thoughts were completely out of control. It was as if my thoughts had a will of their own. I could think of nothing but dread. My phobias had become greatly magnified. Fear had possessed my mind and emotions.

Walking to school that next day, I walked as if in a dream and then the panic would start again. It was hard for me to sit in class because of the panic and distorted thinking--I would run out to the bathroom. Where could I be safe? I didn't want anyone to know the state I was in, so I did my best to hide it.

My life became a terrible mess. At school, I spoke to a psychologist but he didn't help much. Every time I mentioned my mother, I would cry uncontrollably and had to lie down on a couch in the room. I could barely function.

Over the days and weeks that followed, I began to have suicidal thoughts, depression, and despair. It was as if I was stuck on a bad drug trip--caught in the middle of a nightmare. I saw no way out of my pain. I hoped that I would just wake up one morning and be normal again, but I never did. School, housework, childcare, and cooking continued—and so did the pain; the same old questions about life and death still haunted me.

One day I went in to see one of my advisers at school. He was a kind man with whom I had confided previously. I told him I was feeling very out of sorts and nothing seemed real. I asked him if he could help me and he asked if I would like to speak to a woman he knew; he said she might be able to help me. Nodding my head, I told him yes, I would speak to anyone who would listen and could help me.

Thinking back, I can trace the hand of God in my life even at this disturbing time. It was He who had assigned a meeting with this lady. That day at school, I waited out front on the grass with my little black dog, Boston. The sky was blue, the grass was green, life around me was as normal as ever, but I remained changed. Then, I saw her walking up the steps to the school campus, a beautiful lady with black hair and a light blue coat. I felt inside that this was the woman with whom I was to talk--and indeed it was. Her name was Shannon. And so, there we were, sitting out under the huge pepper trees, sitting out on the high school campus, with my dog, Boston, lying next to me. I talked, I cried; she talked, I cried; and then, my life was changed again.

Thinking back on these days is never easy for me. Sometimes, I feel a very foreboding feeling as I recall echoes of yesterday. The suffering was so imprinted in my being. But it still is just that, an echo, a memory, a feeling.

And it seems so very long ago.

Chapter 2
A New Beginning

S hannon and I talked for hours that day in front of the high school. She listened as I poured out my heart. I told her everything, my experience, my fears, how my life seemed hopeless. She listened with so much sincere love in her eyes--so much compassion that it drew me in. She told me that Jesus Christ could help me, and then she pulled out a small booklet and read it with me. The booklet explained how my sins had separated me from God and that God had sent Jesus to die on the cross for my sins so I could be forgiven and restored to fellowship with Him. Jesus rose again on the third day and He was alive today, ready to give me new life and eternal life in heaven when I died.

When I heard about Jesus being the answer to my problems, something clicked inside my spirit. I knew it was all true; I had been taught about Jesus as a little child, but now He was speaking to me personally. Yes, He could help me; and yes, I wanted to have all my sins forgiven. So I prayed the little prayer in the booklet and asked Jesus to come into my life, to forgive me of my wrong doings, to take control of my life and make me the person He wanted me to be.

Shannon said that since I had been born again by the Holy Spirit, I needed to start growing spiritually. She told me to pray, read the Bible, and go to church. A new chapter began that day. With tears rolling down my cheeks I hugged her; and for the first time I experienced hope. I had the answer to life after death; I had the answer about God being real.

Where do I go from here, I wondered?

In my spirit, I felt a huge change--I became alive to the things of God. The Bible was so full of wonderful words, and the Christians I met had so much love and happiness. I stopped doing things that were wrong; I found the power to do what was right. I then went back to my classes, so I could graduate, and even though I couldn't concentrate at times, God helped me. At that time, I had no idea that years later I would return to school to complete my Bachelor of Arts in Biblical Studies, as well as my Masters in Theological Studies—but God knew.

At home, I also became more loving to my brothers and sisters and obedient to my parents; I really wanted to please God. There was a Christian coffee house I would go to called the "Ark" where songs were sung, cookies were served, the Bible was taught, and where one could feel accepted and loved. I found where I belonged. I even began composing Christian songs on my mother's old four-stringed guitar. My face was aglow with the love of God, and I served as a witness to friends on the high school campus about my new life in Christ.

A few weeks after my conversion, I felt a strong sense of God's call to me to the ministry, and to study and teach the Bible. I would sit in the office at the Ark coffee house and read a big Bible housed there. As I read, I would feel such a powerful pulling and hunger for the Bible that I just knew I had to know more. I also had to share my faith with whoever would listen. When a group from the Ark would go downtown to hand out Bible tracts, I went with them, playing the tambourine and wearing my long dress which was the style back in the 70's. There was a strong sense of joy amidst the fear and panic I was still battling, for although my spirit had been made brand new, I had the same old, broken, tormented mind. However, my hope was ever planted in that day when I would be healed and restored by God. So, I marched ahead like a good little soldier for Jesus Christ.

In my Christian faith, I was learning how to pray, how to study the Bible, memorize Scripture, share my faith with others and so much more. God brought some beautiful Christian people in my life that supported me and encouraged me. This was my new life and I held on with all my might to the hope that one day God would heal my damaged emotions and rearrange my thought patterns so once again I would think normally. Despite my progress, I felt stuck in my inward painful thinking, which seemed to be getting worse.

Chapter 3
A Turn for the Worse

It was apparent to me that something was seriously wrong with my thinking. Day by day would go by and I still didn't experience any kind of peace of mind or freedom from the terror and depression. I sought special prayer and meditated on the Scriptures in the Bible; I tried everything I could think of to change my pattern of thinking--but change would not come.

As I look back on those days, I recall the time I had my wisdom teeth out. It was surgery and back at that time a person could be out of commission for a few weeks. I was a captive to my bed and to the things that went on in my head. So many doubts filled my mind. Doubts about God and Jesus being real, doubts again about life after death, and doubts about my sanity. One day, I could no longer take it and I cried out to God to stop the terrible cloud that continually enveloped my brain. My body was wracked with anxiety and panic--I had replays of the night of the break down--there was no escaping my pain.

I honestly don't know how I would have made it through those days if it hadn't been for God's grace and care. When I would seek out counsel from my Christian mentors, they would tell me to pray and to trust God, to read His Word and to praise Him— counting my blessings would help me come out of my depression. I did all these things; yet, I continued to live in depression, despair always ready to smother me. Then, I began experiencing some new phobias. When I was walking, if I saw a pair of matches on the ground and didn't pick them up, the anxiety inside me escalated. I had to pick them up or I thought it might start a fire and kill people and then it would be my fault. Guilt and irrational fears consumed my daily thinking. When I went to the store to pick up some fruits and vegetables I would imagine that I had something poisonous on my hands that would contaminate the food, so I would wash my hands--but still have that awful nagging thought. I knew these thoughts were irrational, but my fear was so strong it took over my emotions. Obsessive thoughts of cursing and hateful thinking would result in a cycle of guilt and shame on my part, even after I confessed it all. It would just happen over and over again--I had no control even though I didn't want those thoughts at all. No one really knew what I was going through. Some very close friends knew I struggled emotionally, but they didn't know how bad it was.

After I turned nineteen I moved out of my house and in with an older lady who was a strong Christian. God had picked this particular lady just for me because she loved me and was there for me all of the time. Her name was Myra. Myra helped me to keep my faith steady and to never give up on hope. What a special lady she was! At this same time, I started my first real job, being a waitress. It was there I met Ike, my husband of forty years. Although I tried hard at my job, it was too stressful and along with all the other mental problems I was having, it added even more anxiety. So, I had to quit and look for something else.

ROXANNE EILERS

Dear God, when would all this emotional pain stop? When would I feel some real relief? God used me even in my pitiful state of pain. I worked with the junior high girls at the church, played my guitar and sang on the radio, and traveled with a group to Oregon to do a revival. Then, I got a job at a little German pastry shop. This job was mine for quite a few years and it was something I liked to do.

But, my obsessive thinking became worse and I found myself alarmed with fear from the moment I opened my eyes in the morning until the time I hit the pillow at night. The unreal feelings, the inward negative ruminating made my brain feel like it was continually short circuiting. I remember when I would leave after work I would have to turn off the coffee machine and lock the door of the pastry shop. However, even though I did this, even though I checked and double checked, I would worry all night that I didn't turn off the coffee machine and that the place might burn up, or that someone would break in because of my carelessness by not locking up properly. Then every morning when I got there everything was always fine. One would think I would trust myself but I didn't. I had a difficult time trusting God also, but I knew He was my only hope of deliverance, so I hung on to Him as best I could. I hung on to the Scriptures and memorized a lot of them, trying to be transformed by the renewing of my mind.

So many times, I thought I was losing my mind and I would feel the traumatic effects again of the original break down--the shock, the panic. I've heard what I was experiencing referred to as "post traumatic syndrome". Even so, I kept on living and tried to be as "normal" as possible.

Ike and I decided to get married in November 1975, and we moved into a cute apartment we shared. Now, new concerns emerged; the fear of getting pregnant and having a baby weighed upon my mind and raised new questions for me. If I could barely handle myself, how could I raise a child? I had to be sure not to get pregnant, at least not at that time; I was always thinking that mental health and wholeness would be a reality in the future and only then could I have my baby. I adored children but felt I had to wait.

After a year, Ike and I felt God calling us to study for the ministry, so we decided to move to Orange County to attend Vanguard University. We planned to attend a Christian college to be trained for ministry; it was an exciting time for us; it was also a big change to leave the place where I had been born and raised, Palm Springs, California.

After enrolling into college, I questioned my decision. How well could I study with my handicap? Somehow, though I had learned to live with my fears, I had also learned to push them aside long enough to function in my everyday life. However, I had not yet learned how to face my fears, and they were always simmering inside me ready to explode into a repeat of the pattern of the original trauma, given the right circumstances and pressures.

These years were some of the hardest years for me. Ike didn't know just how painful my life was; I didn't tell him much of what was going on inside me. I didn't know what was going on myself. All I knew was that I hurt emotionally all the time. There was a time during chapel at school where I sobbed and sobbed at the altar during the call time of prayer. I felt God had forgotten me and my suffering. Then I heard, almost an audible voice inside me speaking a Scripture to me from Isaiah 49:15: "Can a mother forget the baby at her breast and have no compassion on the child she has borne? Though she may forget, I will not forget you!" I could not believe it! God spoke to me powerfully and confirmed His care for me, His concern for me and my personal struggles. This Scripture carried my faith for a long time.

Another time, I was practicing voice lessons in the music room at school and I cried out to God to use me-- that was my greatest burning desire, for Him to use me in the ministry. I heard that same voice I had heard in chapel and this time He gave me Isaiah 42: 6-7: "I, the Lord, have called you in righteousness; I will take hold of your hand. I will keep you and will make you to be a covenant for the people and a light for the Gentiles, to open eyes that are blind, to free captives from prison and to release from the dungeon those who sit in darkness." This was His great promise to me, that He would indeed use me to touch the lives of many people. And, that I would not be trying to make myself fit and ready for service, but that He, Himself, would make me into that person. I would be helping other people to be free from their oppression and darkness; I would bring them Jesus, the One who could save and heal them. However, He also told me that I would have to have spiritual heart surgery done first. I knew right away what He was talking about. I needed to face my fears and emotional pain and find the underlying cause of them.

Although God was using me in different ways at the time, I knew He was preparing me for something greater in the future, but a measure of healing had to come first before I could be in the place where God could really use me to help others heal.

During school, God really had His hand on me because I studied hard in spite of my illness, and I graduated *Magna Cum Laude*; I also received an award for having the highest Grade Point Average in my junior class. What a miracle! As I look back on those days God brought me through—I reflect how amazing He was!

Chapter 4
Spiritual Heart Surgery

After graduating from college, Ike and I moved back to the desert where we planted a church. We were excited to see what God would reap in our little church and looked forward to growing along with it. I led worship with my guitar, ministered to those who came, and helped my husband with other church related duties. On the outside, it appeared I had it all together, but God and I knew that my symptoms of fear, obsessive thinking and compulsiveness were getting worse because of the stress I was under and the fact I had buried everything so far down that it was now all beginning to erupt like a volcano. I kept it quite hidden by excusing myself to the bathroom when I felt panicky or smiling my way through. I had to act as if I knew what I was doing as a pastor's wife.

Hiding was the worst thing I could have done, but I was too embarrassed to share my struggles with anyone for fear they would judge me as a pastor's wife--I *should* have it together. What would they think of me? *I would not be a good example*. What pressure I was under during those years,

Finally, I began to be swallowed deeper and deeper into severe depression. I could barely function, yet somehow, I managed to get things done. One day, as I was in the back yard of the house we were renting, I poured some soapy water that I had used to wash the floors out on the grass. My mind went crazy with irrational fear--as it would often those days. My neighbors had some fruit trees on the other side of the wall where I emptied the soapy water. The first thought was that the water would poison the trees and if they ate the fruit they would die, and of course, it would be my fault. You might think, *Really!--consider the stupidity of those thoughts*. But nothing helped—my thoughts were so confused I couldn't rationalize them. I was getting desperate.

I finally sought some professional help. Being a pastor's wife I was afraid that everyone in the community would know my weaknesses if I went to see a therapist; this is what kept me from going to see one. But it was time. God again had orchestrated the perfect person to help me face my fears, so I went to see the therapist. One night, as I sat in her office, I felt so ill. Things had gotten out of hand. When I drove, I was afraid that I had hit someone who wasn't even there. I continued to imagine things that were not true. A part of me knew that these imaginations were not true but I could not shake them. I was living in a world of unreality. When I would write a check, I was overcome with the fear that I had written something terrible and evil. I told the therapist these things, fearing she would really think I had gone off the deep end and put me into a hospital, but she didn't. She just listened, loved me, and firmly challenged me to grow.

This woman who was to be my therapist for the next eight years was truly sent by God. She reminded me of that woman who came to see me on the high school campus. Mary was a beautiful, godly Christian therapist who had so much love and compassion. She did not condemn nor judge me. She told me I was sick and that we needed to work hard to get out of the deep pit I was in. At this point, I was so afraid I didn't have the strength to pull myself out. I was falling deeper into unreality and depression. She mentioned medicine and I grew even more terrified. I refused to take medicine; then she mentioned something about shock treatments if I continued to be unresponsive to therapy. Dear God, was this all really happening to me?

Week after week, month after month, I went to see Mary. We began to work through my childhood and the experiences that I needed to address. Forgiving became a crucial necessity for me. So, I worked on forgiving my parents, brothers and sisters for anything I held against them. I had to choose to forgive those who had wounded me deeply. This was God's way. I cried--she hugged me--I forgave--she hugged me--I cried some more--she prayed for me. I grasped on to what little reality I had left and held on to the hand of God. I had to make it through.

I had to get well. I worked extremely hard--it was very difficult. This was the heart surgery that God had told me that I would go through when I was in college. It hurt! But I hung on, with the grace of God, and set my face like a flint like Mary suggested. She told me giving up was not an option. I had to fight the good fight of faith and lay hold on life. No matter what, I would make it through with God's help.

Many days passed, followed by years. I kept journals on the life skills and truths I was learning. I was beginning to grow up, finally, at the age of 39. One day, Mary asked me when I was going to try for a child. That struck a panic button, and I was terrified. I said I would--soon. I was not, however, where I wanted to be yet; I felt I was not stable enough emotionally. What if I had panic attacks being pregnant? What if emotionally I couldn't take it and had a replay of the break down? What if I would eat something, or do something that would hurt the baby? Dear God, help me! We talked endlessly about these things. Facing fears that I had, she talked me through them. I was also learning coping skills and the right way of thinking. Right thinking, I found, was vitally important in my walk to wellness.

Sometime during these sessions, I made the decision to step out in faith. Ike and I attempted to conceive a baby and miraculously I became pregnant the first time we tried, after nineteen years of marriage. God gave me special grace when I was pregnant, and I found that when I pulled myself to stay in my present, I could handle things, but if I borrowed tomorrow's worries and cares I would panic. Mary gave me important tools to combat and deal with my fears at the time. She began to work with me on helping me change my thought patterns. During those days God was with me in a gentle yet strong way. And so, after the allotted time, I had our baby, Joseph David Walter Eilers, on June 5, 1993 at the age of 39 years, with Mary and Ike beside me holding my hand.

Now, the challenge of raising my baby was set before me--new adventures to experience and more growing up to do. I was maintaining myself at the time; I had some clear periods where I could keep fears away, at least in the background of my mind, and I fought hard to bring my thoughts back to reality and what was going on in my present. I worked hard on living in my present even though the obsessions were always lurking somewhere in the background of my mind.

At this time, Ike and I were no longer pastoring the little church, and we were attending a church up the street where we lived. I loved having Joseph and caring for him kept me busy and wonderfully occupied. My thoughts began to focus more on him than on my fearful thinking.
However, after a while I began to regress again.

Soon, my depression affected my entire body as well as my mind; I would lie in bed, lose my appetite, tremble and shake. I was still in therapy, one-on-one as well as group therapy, but after working through so many issues in my life, I still found myself struggling with the same painful thinking. I was feeling desperate again and I decided to see a psychiatrist. This would indeed be a new journey for me.

Chapter 5
A New Journey

Waiting to see the psychiatrist, I feared the worst. My fear was that she would truly find me crazy, hopeless, sedate me and put me in the hospital. (I had thought of putting myself in the hospital.) Her name was Dr. Markley, a sweet, petite woman with blond hair. She ushered me into her office and presented several questions to answer, which I answered the best I could. We talked and I told her of my symptoms. Then she told me something that was about to change my life. She said that it sounded like I had what was called Obsessive, Compulsive Behavior, also known as OCD, along with severe depression and anxiety. I finally had a name for all the suffering I had experienced. I asked her if it was because of the earlier breakdown and she said that was a strong possibility. I believe my whole mental chemistry had been altered after the breakdown and I ended up with mental illness.

I was relieved and disturbed while still in denial of the whole thing. You mean I am mentally ill? Just the sound of those words caused me to become frightened. Like so many people, I stereo-typed how a mentally ill person looked and behaved. It couldn't be me--I had a baby, I was a pastor's wife, I ministered to ladies, sang solos, played my guitar, I was intelligent! But, this *was* me, and I had to face the reality of myself once again.

Dr. Markley told me that she had many patients who had these symptoms and that medicine helped tremendously. Finally, at this point in my life, I decided to try the medicine. To me, it now made sense. Just as a diabetic needs insulin to treat his or her disorder, so one whose chemistry is unbalanced also needs to take the appropriate medicine. Apprehensively, I said I would try. And so, I continued my journey into emotional growth and wholeness.

I would like to interject here a little bit of information about Obsessive, Compulsive Behavior. In his book, *Brain Lock*, Dr. Jeffrey Schwartz explains a lot about this illness. He says that OCD is a "medical condition" related to a chemical imbalance in the brain. Obsessions are thoughts that won't go away; they cause fear and torment to the mind. Compulsions are the things we do over and over again, trying to get rid of the uncomfortable feelings that the obsessive thoughts produce (Schwartz 1996). If you are suffering with this disease or if you know of someone who is, I highly recommend this book, *Brain Lock*. This handbook has helped me to work through and control my own struggle with this illness. It is a self-treatment on how to change the chemistry of the brain using four main concepts. However, at this point in my story, I did not have this book and did not understand much about my condition.

I continued my therapy with Mary, and began my new treatment with my psychiatrist. It seemed like forever for the medicine to begin to work. And it worked up to a point. Along with the anti-depressant, I found I also needed something to calm me down inside, and a sleeping aid. So, there I was at 43 years old, receiving all the treatment I could for my disease of OCD and depression/anxiety. However, it wasn't until I began to read up on these diseases that I began to understand them and how they could be managed (as mentioned above). I studied and read about OCD and what the symptoms were. I learned that it was called the "doubting disease"; I began to understand why I had so many doubts and why I had difficulty trusting myself. I had to learn to trust myself and my abilities; I also had to learn to trust God by using my will instead of my emotions because my emotions were all over the place. My life was one big doubting match. I learned from Hannah Whitall Smith's book, *The Christian's Secret to a Happy Life*, to use my will to believe God and to trust Him. I learned that if I chose to place my will over to the believing side, the side of faith, eventually my emotions would follow.

The meds helped my depression and OCD to a certain degree, and I began to continue to acquire tools on how to handle my emotional handicap. I also found that there were others who suffered as I did, and had similar irrational thoughts. I was not alone in my suffering. I knew God was with me, but I also needed to be reassured that there were other human beings with whom I could relate. Finding them was a tremendous encouragement to me.

I began to sing on the worship team for ladies' ministries, and teach Bible studies; I even wrote a study that I taught. I homeschooled my son at the time, so my life was busy and full. However, it wasn't until after changing my meds to more effective ones that I began to feel significant relief from my symptoms. And with my new understanding of my illness I knew what to expect. Panic no longer controlled my emotions. I learned how to combat and overcome the OCD, even when it was screaming to erupt and take power over my thinking. Very gradually, my thoughts had turned outward, and my mind began to heal. I began to connect with reality because I had made Jesus Christ my strong tower and hiding place; I was feeling safer and more secure with my life and living in the world. I learned how to trust God more and to give Him all the things that caused me to fret and worry. Later, I also decided to go back to school to earn my Masters in Theological Studies. With fresh confidence, we moved our family, which included our son and my mother-in-law, to Orange County where Ike and I went back to Vanguard University and began to work on our MTS.

I have often asked myself why I had to suffer so unreasonably. It was excruciating. However, God has performed a tremendous amount of healing inside my mind and spirit. I no longer have the tormenting flashbacks of the break down. I no longer allow my disease to run my life. I am not afraid to leave the safety of my home, and I am no longer paralyzed with fear of traveling. God is so wonderful because He always gives us things that will help us tolerate our trying times. In my case, God has given me the gifts of song, art, and writing. These helped and comforted me during my season of suffering.

God is at work in my life, empowering me to victory. I can focus on Him more clearly now and enjoy His love and grace. Periods of peace and joy are much more frequent; depression is held at bay and I feel free to be all that God has called me to be. I admit I am a late bloomer, but God carefully orchestrated every detail of my life, even my suffering, to bring me to where I am today.

The encouraging people that were brought into my life at just the right times, the therapy, the medicine, the books, the experiences--His grace and strength were all part of His special plans for me. The Lord has taught me so much during my years of suffering and that is the reason I have written this book--in order to encourage those who are in a season of suffering and cannot make sense out of it, as well as those who feel hopeless and in despair.

The lessons I have learned and am learning are adventures in themselves, knowing that God's hand is always with me, guiding me through every circumstance and situation. He has truly worked out all these difficulties that were fighting me, for my good and His glory. In the following pages are some of the principles that the Lord has taught me--truths on how to go through times of intense suffering and to keep holding on to hope.

You see, we are all plodding along on our own personal journeys, learning valuable lessons as we go. Are we willing to follow God, even through the most severe sufferings and discomfort? Are we willing to learn how to live during great turmoil and still proclaim that He is God? Are we willing to share our lives with others so that they might be encouraged to make that next step in the dark? God has asked me to go down these particular roads of suffering to make me into broken bread to feed others. The glory part of it is that He has brought me out on the other side of suffering and invited me to walk with Him in grace and glory. However, that does not mean I don't have bad days or struggle with my illness at times, nor am I through with suffering. I know there will always be those seasons of suffering in different degrees.

Today, I am excited for what God is doing at this moment and will be doing in my future. He has made a way for me to do my art, write, sing, speak and travel; and above all to reach out to people with the message of hope and deliverance. God is doing what He promised He would do, and that is, make me into a vessel fit to do His work. He has been so faithful in His ongoing work in me, converting to good use all those things that seemed to be against me--those things that could have destroyed me. God intervened and helped me to turn that corner where I finally embraced a steady hope. My dear friend, if God did this for me, I am persuaded He will do the same for you. I know from experience that God can help us, preserve us and present us before the Father whole, lacking in nothing.

Pressing upon my heart has been the desire to share not only my story but truths that the Lord has taught me through my difficult years. There are so many things that the Lord has taught and shown me, but I have condensed some of these truths in a way that I believe will be easy to access and understand. So, in the following chapters we will be looking at seven concepts that can help us to keep our hope strong during times of adversity.

Chapter 6
Seven Truths

As I mentioned before, God has taught me so many treasured truths and in the following chapters I will be sharing some of these with you. These truths have helped me to keep holding on to hope in my season of suffering, and I pray that they will encourage and help you in your time of need as well. I have seven points that I will be talking about. Each point will have some questions for you to ponder and a little Bible study if you would like to dig deeper on the subject matter. You will find the answers to most of the questions in the chapter itself. Enjoy! To begin, here are the seven concepts that God has given me:

1. Know God Personally.
2. Develop a Right Mindset.
3. Have Encouraging Hand-Holders.
4. Pray Always in Everything.
5. Let God Use You and Your Gifts.
6. Get Away With God.
7. Let God Work While You Trust, Rest and Wait.

1) Know God Personally

J.I. Packer, in his book, *Knowing God*, asks why we were created. He answers that question by saying that we were created to get to know God. He further asks what should be our aim in life. And he answers again, that we should make our aim to know God personally. His final question is what does it mean when Jesus gives us eternal life? He answers by saying that eternal life is to know God (Packer 1973).

God has invited us to have an intimate relationship with Him through His son, Jesus. God has invited us to know Him personally, but we must make this choice. His Word, the Bible, tells us all about Him and His love for us. It tells us how we can know Him and walk with Him in this life, preparing us for the next. So, in getting ready to set our hearts on persevering unto hope, the very first thing we must do is to know God personally. How hard is this?

We can learn about who God is and what He is like by reading the Bible. The Bible tells us that God's love for us is higher than the heavens, and that His mercy towards us is very great. God is also our personal creator, and He is the sustainer of all things that exist. But, we are alienated from God because we have sinned and chosen to go our own way instead of God's way. We are separated from God. "For the wages of sin is death, but the gift of God is eternal life in Christ Jesus our Lord" (Rom. 6:23). Jesus died on the cross and rose again from the dead to take away our sins and to deliver us out of the power of darkness. Thus, we must be reconciled to God through the way

Hope In A Season Of Suffering

He has provided, which is through His only Son, Jesus Christ. The Bible says "to all who did receive Him, to those who believed in His name, He gave the right to become children of God" (John 1:12).

Jesus came down to earth, to bring us back to God and to give us eternal life. The Scriptures tell us, "For God so loved the world that He gave His only begotten son that whosoever believes in Him will not perish but have everlasting life" (John 3:16).

It is wonderful to know God and to walk with Him every day. To know Him personally is something that you simply make the decision and choice to do. If you have never given your life over to the care and keeping of the Lord Jesus Christ, now is a good time. Today is the day of Salvation. If you believe in the Lord Jesus, you will be saved and brought into a relationship with God (Acts 16:31).

If you pray the prayer of faith and you mean it, God will forgive you of all your sins, send His Holy Spirit to come and live within your heart, and He will make Himself known to you. He will become your unmovable foundation---Christ Jesus being the chief corner stone upon which you can build your hope.

Do you want to know God and be part of the family of God? Do you want to be a child of God? Or are you already a Christian with knowledge of the Lord, but need to rededicate your life to Him? You can pray this simple prayer of faith right now with me. This prayer is like the one that I prayed while I was sitting on the high school campus many years ago when I gave my life to Christ and entered into a relationship with God.

ROXANNE EILERS

Dear Father, I come to You today and I know that I have sinned. Please forgive me for breaking Your laws and going my own way. But I believe that Jesus loves me and died for my sins and that He rose again from the dead. I ask You to come into my life right now, take control of the throne of my life, take the reins of my life, and make me the person You want me to be. From this day forward I will live for You. Help me, Father, now to grow in knowing You. Thank you for saving me, in Jesus Name, I pray, Amen.

After inviting Christ into your life, it is vital that you begin to grow spiritually in the Lord through prayer, fellowship with other believers, reading and studying of the Bible and being a witness for Him. A good place to start is to find a good church that teaches what the Bible says.

Now, I would like to say something about the foundation our life is built upon, because knowing God is a big part of that foundation. How do we know what kind of foundation we are building? I have found that in times of stress and trial, the core of who we really are and what we believe about ourselves, our situation, others, and God, always surfaces to the top. If we don't have a strong anchor or foundation on which to place our hope, we will find ourselves drifting, blown about unmercifully by the drowning waves of trouble, depression, and confusion. So, what kind of foundation do we need?

I believe that it is extremely important that our foundation be a true solid rock for the soul. The Bible states that this Rock is Jesus Christ, the Son of the living God. I call it the *basic* foundation on which to build my life and faith. There is no other God, there is no other security that is lasting, but in the arms of the God of the Bible. Other people, and objects, will disappoint us; they cannot hold us up through the fiery trials that we experience. Oh, they can help us and be somewhat of a support, but we need a true foundation that is unmovable, unshakeable, and unchangeable, a foundation that gives us hope, that is an anchor of the soul both sure and steadfast. As you come to know God and build on His foundation, He will give you what is necessary in order for you to have true perseverance to hope in the face of difficulty that goes beyond your own ability and strength. We need to be taught by God how to persevere His way, for His way brings victory and solid growth.

Knowing God personally is the first step in being able to have hope in a season of suffering. It is the most important of all steps because all the other concepts we need to adhere to are built upon this basic foundation of faith.

The Scriptures tell us in Jeremiah 9:23, "Thus saith the LORD, Let not the wise man glory in his wisdom, neither let the mighty man glory in his might, let not the rich man glory in his riches; but let him that glorieth glory in this, that he understandeth and knoweth Me"(KJV). Be happy and rejoice that you can know God through His Son, Jesus Christ our Lord!

ROXANNE EILERS

Discussion Questions:

1. What should be our aim in this life?
2. What happens to the core of who we really are during times of stress and trial? Do you agree with this? Why or Why not?
3. Do you feel like you have a strong foundation under you right now? What is it?
4. What are some false foundations?
5. What does the Bible say our foundation should be and why?
6. Have you made Christ your foundation?
7. What are some of the ways you can grow?

Bible Study:

1. Read 1 Corinthians 15:3-4. What did Jesus do for us?
2. According to John 1:12, what do we need to do in order to have the right to become a child of God?
3. In 1 John 5:11-12, what has God given those who have His Son?
4. And then 1 John 5:13, if we believe in the Name of the Son of God, what assurance may we have?

Now, as a Christian, grow in the knowledge, grace, and love of the Lord. Become rooted and grounded in Him and get to know Him more intimately. Choose to please Him and to walk in His ways as He reveals them to you in His Word, the Bible.

2) **Develop a Right Mindset.**

This concept is vital and I can't stress it enough, for how we think is how we will deal and cope with the sufferings we encounter. In order to persevere in our suffering, we must have the right mindset to think about what's going on around and in us in the light of the truth. How do we know what the truth is?

The truth is found in the pages of the Bible. Thus, we need to study in order to know what the Bible says about matters of the heart and of life. We need to ask ourselves, how would Jesus think about this or that? What things does He ask us to do, or to change in our lives? How does He ask us to walk and what does He ask us to think about? For example, the Bible tells us in Philippians 4:8-9 what things we are to think about—the good, wholesome, and pure. How we handle the difficult moments that come to us is greatly influenced by our attitude and mindset—whether we will believe the truth or the false lies.

When I first started therapy, a book that really was an effective instrument for me to develop a right mindset was *Telling Yourself the Truth* by William Backus and Marie Chapian. I read and re-read this book and found the truths I needed to refute the lies that were constantly bombarding me. They talk about "misbeliefs" or lies that we tell ourselves as a cause for most of the emotional disturbances we encounter. What we think can make us sick mentally--or make us healthy. They also say that the lies that come to us are straight from hell itself, and the devil wants to get us so enmeshed in ourselves, with our emotions and the misbeliefs we are holding, that we cannot hear God's voice.

Just the lie of saying, "I am no good" can work its way into your mind and heart and cause damage and negative results. Backus and Chapian give many examples of what they discuss, and they say that we can change and refute the misbeliefs we hold, that is, with God's help (Backus/Chapian 1980). We can do all things through Christ who gives us the strength (Philippians 4:13). To summarize, what we think is vitally important to our mental health, and having the right mindset is a major part of being able to hold on to our hope in times of suffering.

It's easy to allow our emotions to dominate the way we perceive and handle situations. This can and often does lead us to wobbly faith, and discouragement. But we don't have to be blown about by our emotions of the moment; we can stand on what we know is true and reject false thinking. We can choose to believe and walk in faith using our will in the matter—God empowering us.

Tell yourself, because you have God in your life, you *can* handle this and because you have His Word, you *can* arm yourself spiritually and emotionally. You can think the way God wants you to think with the Holy Spirit's empowerment. According to Romans 12:2, we are to be transformed by the renewal of our minds. You can have the mind of Christ.

Hope In A Season Of Suffering

Now let us focus on some mindsets that I believe will encourage and strengthen you in your journey into hope.

Mindset Number One: *Suffering is always for a specific purpose of God.*

Something is being produced through our suffering; therefore, it is valuable—we are being changed by it (Yancey1977). No suffering is in vain if we let God work in us and in our situation. There are always lessons to be learned from what we experience in our lives, and there is always a purpose that God has in mind. Some of these purposes are: to learn more about God and His ways, to be comforted so that we can comfort others, to develop character and perseverance, to be able to teach others, and to refine our faith.

When we learn about God and His ways we bring change into our lives. He tells us in His Word to live our lives in holiness and be a light in our dark generation. When we get off the path, hardship brings us back to hearing God's voice and finding out what He again desires for us. We are challenged to choose His way rather than our own way—whether in deed or attitude. In my own life, I have had to choose to obey God or go my own way. My way would bring about increased suffering and confusion, so I chose early to go God's way and accept His will for me at that moment. In accepting His will, I know I will have victory eventually.

ROXANNE EILERS

Another purpose for our suffering is that we can learn to be a comfort to others. In studying God's Word, we can find comfort in our pain and answers to our problems. When we are in suffering mode, God knows that we hurt, and He is the God of all comfort who comforts us in all our afflictions. The Bible tells us in 2 Corinthians 1:3-4, "Praise be to the God and Father of our Lord Jesus Christ, the Father of compassion and the God of all comfort, who comforts us in all our troubles, so that we can comfort those in any trouble with the comfort we ourselves receive from God." If we draw near to God, and draw comfort from His Word, and allow His people to comfort us, then we will be learning how to comfort others. When we find comfort while we are in our misery, we learn how to make others feel a little better when they are in their valley of trial and affliction also.

Listening to worship music, thinking upon Scripture, praying, soaking in God's presence and love, sharing with other Christians, doing things for others, knowing that things always pass and things will get better, getting enough sleep, reading a good book, exercising, treating yourself to something you like are some ways to find comfort when we are feeling down. We can encourage others with such truths as we learn and grow; we can hold out hope to them.

Again, a big reason God allows suffering is to develop our inward person. Our character desperately needs to be developed and refined. We need to be changed because left to ourselves we have the natural tendency to be self-centered, easily annoyed, vain, proud, and boastful. We also tend to want life to be easy and without troubles. How shallow we would be if we had no troubles. *Suffering either makes us humble and pliable or hard and unyielding.*

All kinds of attitudes come forth from our hearts when we are under the fires of trial. Sometimes pressure brings out the worst in us, but if we allow God to work in us He will bring out the fruit of the Spirit. God's Word and the Holy Spirit are two agents that God uses to construct character in us. The Word of God reveals to us how we are to live and the Holy Spirit empowers us to be obedient to God's Word. Through the exercise of suffering we learn to forgive, develop perseverance, and to be kind and understanding of others.

I remember when my mother-in-law came to live with us. She had a broken neck and needed tending to; she needed patient care and a tender touch. Boy! Was I in for a surprise with the attitudes that were revealed in my heart as I took care of her! She lived with us for almost four years and I had to battle with resentment, impatience, selfishness and other inward attitudes. Through those years, however, God taught me so many things, such as perseverance, kindness, patience, and forgiveness. However, I know I will always have to learn to exercise these disciplines repeatedly in my daily living, on my journey of life. The Bible tells us that "No discipline seems pleasant at the time, but painful. Later, however, it produces a harvest of righteousness and peace for those who have been trained by it" (Hebrews 12:11).

Such Scriptures as 2 Corinthians 4:16-18, tell us that the affliction we find ourselves in is but a light affliction, compared to eternity and God has the overall big picture in mind. Our outward person is perishing, and we see this happening as we grow older with age, but our inward person, our spiritual being inside, is being renewed day by day. Wow! That means our spirit is getting stronger and stronger and when it is time for us to leave this world we will be ready to embrace the invisible realm, which will become visible, the spiritual realm which is the true reality where God has prepared a glorious life for us.

Suffering refines our faith. Of what is our faith made? Will it stand up under hardship or will it crumble? When God seems to be silent and the situation remains the same, when the trials keep coming one after another, will my faith stay steady or will it falter? Steady faith does not just happen, it is developed. God calls the "trying of our faith" much more precious than gold that perishes (1 Peter 1:6-7). Faith pleases God and He is a rewarder of those who possess such faith. In Hebrews 11:6 we read that "without faith it is impossible to please God, because anyone who comes to Him must believe that He exists and that He rewards those who earnestly seek Him."

There was an incident many years ago that caused me to take a stand, to believe and to trust God. I was on my way to see my psychiatrist because I was suffering with intense emotional pain and depression. The pain was so bad that I felt desperate and needed relief--fast. Fear, panic, and replays of the breakdown overwhelmed me and the thoughts that were forcing their way into my mind were terrifying. The enemy of my soul took advantage of my weakness and shouted lies into my ears. "This will never change. You will never get well. You will just end up in the hospital drugged up. Just kill yourself." I remember I cried out to God and a Bible Scripture came into my mind. "Though He slay me, yet will I trust Him" (Job 13:15 KJV). Though God allows me to go through the fires of hell on earth I will still hold fast to Him. I began to say it aloud, then louder and louder, and I resisted the devil that day through the power of the Lord. God brought me through that day as I trusted Him moment by moment. My faith stood the test.

Looking back on my own life I see how my faith has grown each time I chose to put my trust in God and His Word. Where I could have worried and doubted in a circumstance, I had the choice to trust God, even if this meant trusting repeatedly, pulling myself back up and standing in faith once again. It is an exercise of the spirit, and faith does become stronger as we purpose to use it.

Discussion Questions:

1. What is Mindset #1? Write it out.
2. In order to persevere in our suffering what is one of the things we must have?
3. What are some of the purposes of suffering?
4. How can we find comfort in our pain? What are some of the ways we can find comfort?

5. Suffering makes us___and___or___and___. (Fill in the blanks.)
6. What are the two agents God uses to construct character in us?
7. What refines our faith?
8. Why does our faith need refining?
9. How do you think God rewards those who walk in faith?

<u>Bible Study</u>

1. Look up Hebrews 12:11. After suffering is past, what will it have produced for us?
2. How are we to view our affliction according to 2 Corinthians 4:17-18?
3. According to Romans 5: 1-5 what should our daily perspective be when we are in a season of suffering and grief? What does suffering produce?

Mindset Number Two: *Suffering will not last forever: there is an end to our suffering.*

"How long will this pain go on? I can't take any more of this. It hurts too much. When will these clouds lift?" The Bible tells us that suffering comes in seasons. Seasons in our life come when we need them to come. 1 Peter 1:6 says, "In this ye greatly rejoice, though now for a season (a little while) if need be, ye are in heaviness through manifold trials" KJV (parentheses added). Most of us need this "little while" or "season" of suffering to grow and become the beautiful person we were meant to be. Here is the good news—seasons change. We have winter, spring, summer and fall throughout the days of our lives.
Some say that the winters in their lives are the most trying times; winters are quiet, sometimes a lonely season. Spring is a time of renewal and refreshment, and summer is a time of growing and stretching. Fall is a time to let go of the old and put on and practice the new. For the last two weeks, I think I have been in a summer where my faith is expanding and growing stronger. Since it is the trials that make my faith grow, I can't wait to see the fruit that will be produced by all this stretching! I can see that fall is around the corner and this encourages me because I will be putting into practice all the things I am learning.

Different people view the seasons of life in a variety of ways. A good book on the seasons of life is *Growing Strong in the Seasons of Life* by Charles R. Swindoll. He writes in-depth about the different seasons—it really is an excellent book. Which season are you in right now? Ask God to show you what He is up to in your particular season of life; journal it in your notebook. God is faithful to bring you through each season every time it comes around. I know! I have watched God at work in my own life.

God's Word tells us our affliction is but for a moment. We can stand it one moment at a time. A moment is not forever. Our sufferings and unpleasant times will not last forever and we can tolerate feeling uncomfortable for a defined period in order to achieve a higher gain in the future. I remember when my therapist told me this truth; I hurt so badly but I kept saying to myself, *I can go through this—I can stand anything for a period of time. I won't die—this will pass. There are people who need me—places to go— things to do in the future. God has a plan and a purpose and He knows what is needed in this situation. God will answer my prayers.*

Knowing and believing these truths have seen me through and given me strength in many times of great stress, trial and pain. When I was battling my emotional fears, when I went through labor and delivery of my baby, after my sister died with cancer, when my mother-in-law lived with us, when struggling with financial pressures, when I was in school working on my Master's in Theological Studies, when my father passed away with cancer, when my brother went to prison convicted of murder, when my son was battling addictions, when my brother-in-law shot his wife, then himself, when I would think of my other brother living on the streets---these are just some of the times I kept this way of thinking in the forefront of my mind. In fact, I think this way now in my present; it arms me and assists me when I feel I can't go through something that I need to go through. God tells us to think on things that are true and good; we do have a choice.

You see, there are healthy ways of thinking about our suffering. Remember, we *can* find answers and healthy ways of handling ourselves. The Lord will guide and lead us to where we can find help coping with our suffering. We are never to be harsh with or hurt ourselves in any way, rather we are to be gentle and patient with ourselves. I know this is easier said than done, but at least the truth behind it is a base for our beliefs about ourselves. The Lord says to love ourselves as we love our neighbor. How would you treat your neighbor?

Will we apply what God's Word says about us? You say "I can't!" He says you *can* do all things through Christ who gives you the ability (Philippians 4:13)! Even depression will lift through the correct guidance, a living faith and steady hope. A woman is not pregnant forever, is she? No, she will be delivered and so will we at the appointed time. God knows how much we can bear—He knows and He is gracious with us. If we stay in tune with Him we will know which way to go, what to do, and who to see so our deliverance will come. Remember that "weeping may remain for a night, but rejoicing comes in the morning" (Ps.30:5b). *I hear this Scripture telling me that grief may remain for a season, but joy will come when the season changes.*

ROXANNE EILERS

<u>Discussion Questions:</u>

1. Write out Mindset #2
2. How long will your pain go on?
3. What does a season of suffering mean to you?
4. What is God's perspective on suffering?
5. Even if our afflictions seem to last forever what has God promised us in Philippians 4:13?

<u>Bible Study</u>

1. In 1 Peter 1:6-7 what does Peter say about our suffering?
2. What are we to fill our minds up with in Philippians 4:8? Summarize briefly.
3. In Philippians 3:13-14, what kind of mindset does Paul have that we are to also have?

Mindset Number Three: *God knows whatever we are going through; He is with us in it and gives us the strength to handle it.*

In Psalm 139 we are told that God knows us perfectly. He perceives when we sit down and when we rise. He understands our thoughts from afar. He knows just how we are wired because He wired us that way; He is well acquainted with all our weaknesses and strengths, and He knows just what we need in our lives for us to become the person He created us to be. At times, suffering is part of what we need.

God knows what we are going through. There's a story in the Bible of a man named Job who suffered tremendously. He lost his family, his goods, his wealth, and his health. It happened in this way. Satan came before God and asked permission to touch Job's possessions, his children, and his wealth. God gave him permission. After this shock to Job, Satan came again, before God, and asked permission to ruin Job's health. Again, God gave him permission, but to spare Job's life. The point is that before any of these calamities could even touch Job, God knew about it, and if He knew about it, then He would provide the strength, stability and staying power for Job. He knew that Job would be able to make it through the excruciating sufferings. And Job did make it through and kept his faith in God; therefore, God rewarded him greatly. It was Job's season of suffering. Did God cause the suffering? Absolutely not! God is never the cause of what makes us suffer; rather He is the comforter.

ROXANNE EILERS

According to Jerry Bridges, in his book, *Trusting God Even When Life Hurts*, nothing is too big or too little that God doesn't know about it and rule over it. Even the tiny spider that builds its web on a tree branch is under the care and eye of its maker. We cannot begin to try to figure out what God is doing at times. Sometimes, He allows us to see some things— He lifts the curtain so we can see what He's been up to. However, much of the time we don't see what God intends. But, whatever we go through or encounter, remember, there are no "chance" happenings with God. If God knows all about the small minute happenings of the sparrow (Matt. 10:29-31) how much more does He care and know about us, His children? (Bridges 1988).

Some more thoughts to keep in mind that will help our perspective in the matter of suffering is that we may never *understand* why some things come into our lives, but we *can* trust in God's goodness, love, complete faithfulness, infinite wisdom, and understanding. Sometimes, we cannot make any sense at all out of what is going on. Every corner in our mind, where we search for answers, may seem blocked, and we may feel caught in a confusing maze. We must stop and let God be God. This means finding peace in knowing that He is making something beautiful out of something ugly. He is using everything in our lives to mold us into the image of His son, Jesus. He holds every piece of the puzzle to our life. God's sovereignty is also always at work in our lives, in the lives of others and around us in the world. God is sovereign and does not need to explain His ways and doings to us. He just asks us to trust Him.

So many times, I have asked the Lord why I have had to suffer so much in my life. Sometimes, He has shown me why and He allows me to see behind the curtain of life. This renews my joy and confirms my purpose. However, I know that I will never know all His reasons on this side of heaven, but I am aware that spiritual things are happening, and that God is in charge of my life and knows all about my troubles.

He is with us in our struggles. I also am assured that He is always with me and understands my suffering because we read in the Bible that "In all [our] distress He too was distressed, and the angel of His presence saved [us]" (Isaiah 63:8). This means that God feels what we are feeling. He suffers sorrow with us, and rejoices with us. Another Scripture can be found in the Book of Hebrews 4:15-16: "For we do not have a high priest who is unable to sympathize with our weaknesses, but we have one who has been tempted in every way, just as we are—yet without sin. Let us then approach the throne of grace with confidence, so that we may receive mercy and find grace to help us in our time of need." In other words, Jesus deeply sympathizes with our suffering and affliction, and because He has victoriously overcome, we can approach Him with confidence and find mercy and grace to sustain us in our time of need. He not only feels with us, He has compassion on us.

He gives us strength to go on. God says that you will have just the amount of strength you need for each moment of each day. "As your days, so shall your strength be" (Deut. 33:25). Our days are one at a time, one hour at a time, one moment at a time. We can handle anything moment by moment. Jesus tells us that His grace is sufficient for us, and that His power is perfected in our weaknesses (2 Corin.12:9). This says to me that we have plenty of grace for each of our needs, in the present as well as in the future. Grace means we have all the help and strength we require to be able to manage our affairs and handle the challenges set before us. Also, something supernatural is going on when we suffer—we are not only becoming more like Christ, but Christ's very power can be witnessed in our lives as we trust in Him. "He is our refuge and our strength, our very present help in trouble" (Psalm 46:1). If we call on Him, He will answer us and supply us with whatever we are lacking in order that we might be able to stand and survive spiritually and emotionally.

He will also give us a way of escape so that we will be able to bear up under our trial. God tells us in 1 Corinthians 10:13: "No temptation has overtaken you except what is common to mankind. And God is faithful; He will not let you be tempted beyond what you can bear. But when you are tempted, He will also provide a way out so that you can endure it." He will always show us how to keep on going and to make it through, so leave yourself and your situation as clay in the potter's hand and watch God work! Hold on to your hope!

One last example of God *knowing what we are going through, being with us and strengthening us in our suffering* is found in the Book of Genesis in the

Bible. Genesis, Chapter 21, tells the story of a young maid servant named Hagar who had a son named Ishmael. She was the servant of Sarah, Abraham's wife. In this situation, Hagar was thrown out of the house with her son and was wandering in the desert having run out of water. She placed her son under some bushes because she didn't want to watch him die. God saw their situation, He was aware of their plight, and He had compassion on them. Then, God was moved to do something for them to ease their suffering. The Bible says that God heard the boy crying and He did something about it—He opened Hagar's eyes to see a little well of water to drink from. Hagar filled the water bottle and gave it to her son and he revived. Hagar and Ishmael lived because God cared and was with them in their suffering. The Lord saw them; He heard them; and He acted and gave them renewed strength for the journey.

Love sees, hears, and does something. The same happens in our lives when we cry out to God. He is there for us and hears us and I *know* He will, without a doubt, do something for us in our situation. And, if we will open up our eyes, we will see that God has provided something just for us in order to meet our present need and to give us strength.

Dear One, what is happening in your life right this moment? What trial, what trauma, what conflicts, what troubles, what sufferings? If you belong to the Lord through faith in Jesus Christ, whatever comes into your life is not a surprise to God. Whatever it is, whether through no fault of your own, whether through mistakes, a fallen world, or sin, God will work it out for His purpose by His own loving hand. Perhaps He will build your character or prove your faith and allegiance to Him, or prepare you for your next assignment, or perhaps He will open a whole new door that you never knew existed---God knows the why and the purpose. Sometimes He reveals this to us, sometimes He doesn't, but overall, He will intimately assist us to walk our journey on earth with victories won, so we can ultimately bring the glory to Him.

I honestly believe that when suffering and trials come around in our lives, they *become* God's will for working good in us. What about my situation you ask? I lost a child, or I have cancer, or my brother committed suicide, or I battle with alcohol, or I lost my husband in a freak accident, or I have a son who is on drugs, or I lost my job and the rent is due—just to name a few. Does God cause these tragedies? Absolutely not! As I said previously, we live in a fallen world where things are not perfect and things go wrong. We also make unwise choices, and mistakes. However, God can use these all for His own good purposes for our life. God can and will take whatever terrible things happen in our lives and will *blend them in with other favorable things* and will cause everything to work together for our good and His glory (Rom. 8:28). It is His plan for us to always rise above our circumstances and to experience life to the fullest. Bad things will happen but good comes from the hand of God.

<u>Discussion Questions:</u>

1. Write out mindset # Three.
2. What does God know about us?
3. Why is suffering allowed into our lives?
4. What will God give us to make it through?

<u>Bible Study</u>

1. Read Luke 22:31-32.
2. Who wants to sift Simon Peter's faith? What does Jesus say?
3. When have you felt like Hagar, the maid servant, that life was hopeless?
4. Did you call on God? How did He answer you?
5. Job was considered by God to be an upright man. In 1 John 1:5-7, how does God want us to walk?
6. What do you think this has to do with our attitude of mind?
7. How do we refute the lies the enemy shouts in our ears (1Peter 5:8-9)?
8. What does Romans 8:28 also give us the assurance of?

ROXANNE EILERS

Mindset Number Four: *When we suffer we are compelled to learn the Word of God, cling to God and to go deeper in our relationship with Him.*

Our need for God becomes desperate as we find ourselves backed into a corner. In order to survive, we must allow ourselves to fall into His arms and hold on to what He has promised in the Bible. He is teaching us obedience through His Word and through the things we suffer. His Word keeps us from straying away from the straight and narrow as we allow it to work in us. As we study what God says about our situation, what He will do, and what we are to do, we have some direction to our lives. We are not just going around in circles. God says that we are to hide His Word in our hearts and meditate upon it day and night until it becomes a part of us (Psalm 1). His words are to abide in us and we are to abide in them (John 15:7). We also need to know what God thinks about our situation, how He feels about it and what we should do about it. This comes by learning about Him in His Word.

I remember when I was in a constant struggle with my emotional life. I sought out, in God's Word, what He thought and said about this struggle. I found out that God wanted me to have a sound and healthy mind; I read in 2 Timothy 1:7 "For God has not given us the spirit of fear, but of power, love and of a sound mind" (KJV). I found out that He was with me in my suffering and felt deepest sympathy and compassion for me during these struggles. God also wanted to show me how to live free from fear. This was very exciting to me and gave me hope to keep holding on until I was living out my goal.

I would encourage you to memorize portions of the Bible that pertain to your specific need, just like I did when I was suffering so deeply. Even now, when I go through a very trying time, sometimes I write out Scriptures that the Lord gives me, or underline them in my Bible; I meditate upon them. There are particular passages that will encourage and give us hope when we need it. This is the leading and foremost way in which God communicates with us as His children; there are other ways, but our focus in this chapter is on the Word of God as God's main way of reaching us and speaking to us. Listed below are some Scriptures taken from the Psalms that I found to renew my hope and faith, and I pray they will do the same for you.

Psalm 34:4-7 "I sought the Lord, and He answered me; He delivered me from all my fears. Those who look to Him are radiant; their faces are never covered with shame. This poor man called, and the LORD heard him; He saved him out of all his troubles. The angel of the LORD encamps around those who fear Him and He delivers them."

Psalm 27:1, 14 "The LORD is my light and my salvation—whom shall I fear? The LORD is the stronghold of my life—of whom shall I be afraid? Wait for the LORD; be strong and take heart and wait for the LORD."

ROXANNE EILERS

Psalm 4:1 "Answer me when I call to You, my righteous God. Give me relief from my distress; have mercy on me and hear my prayer."

Psalm 5:3 "In the morning, LORD, You hear my voice; in the morning, I lay my requests before You and wait expectantly."

Psalm 18:18-19 "They confronted me in the day of my disaster, but the LORD was my support. He brought me out into a spacious place; He rescued me because He delighted in me."

Psalm 23:1-4 "The LORD is my shepherd, I lack nothing. He makes me lie down in green pastures, He leads me beside quiet waters; He refreshes my soul. He guides me along the right paths for His name's sake. Even though I walk through the darkest valley, I will fear no evil, for You are with me; Your rod and Your staff, they comfort me."

Psalm 32:8 "I will instruct you and teach you in the way you should go; I will counsel you with My loving eye on you."

Psalm 32:7 "You are my hiding place; You will protect me from trouble and surround me with songs of deliverance."

Psalm 40:1-3 "I waited patiently for the LORD; He turned to me and heard my cry. He lifted me out of the slimy pit, out of the mud and mire; He set my feet on a rock and gave me a firm place to stand. He put a new song in my mouth, a hymn of praise to our God. Many will see and fear the LORD and put their trust in Him."

The Word of God is very effective in lifting us out of a pit of despair and depression; but we must choose to believe and live in it.

During times of trial, our hearts are not only compelled to lean on and search out God's Word, but to cling to Him with all of our hearts, to learn of His love, hear His voice, feel His presence, and to go deeper with Him. When we draw close to the Lord and choose to lean upon His everlasting arms there is a sense of security and calmness. Aren't we desperate for His touch? Dear friend, as we push more into Him and who He is, He will not disappoint us. In times of tremendous struggle, temptation, or trial we are spiritually driven toward God. He is our only hope. I find myself in a constant state of communion with God during these times. I find myself crying out for Him to work in a situation, deliver someone from evil, to have mercy on me—there are so many, many prayers of the moment I bring to Him. And when I desperately need to hear a word of encouragement from Him, I know that He will meet me and my need.

God is always asking us to draw near and cling to Him for He is our life and length of days. God told His people, the Israelites, to hold fast to Him and to love Him. In Deuteronomy 30:20, that word "hold fast" in the Hebrew language is *davaq* and means to stick together like glue. God wants us to be stuck to

ROXANNE EILERS

Him through faith in Him. It is our choice to draw close to Him and to go deeper with Him in our lives.

Sometimes, we may be afraid to go deeper in our relationship with God; we may feel that if we do, He will ask us to do something we think is too difficult. This isn't true. God has so much love He wants to pour out on us, and He wants to take us to a place of closeness with Him that we have never experienced before. Maybe you are just abiding in the shallow end of His pool of love and mercy; or perhaps you are in the process of treading water and trying to keep afloat in your relationship with the Savior.

There is an article in the blog section of the *Sacus* "Sabah Adventist Association of College and University Students," dated Sunday, Jan. 24, that was interesting and concise. This article lists five ways to go deeper with God.

The *first step* is to move towards God; take that risk of getting to know and want Him more. Wade out to where Jesus is—He is as near as your heartbeat, and He will meet you where you are. Make a choice to go deeper with God and ask Him to continue to ignite a greater desire for Him within your heart.

The *second step* is to make time for God in your life. Life is so busy for all of us and we can exhaust ourselves trying to just meet our daily schedules. But, in the midst of all our hustle and bustle, we must and need to make time for God. I will talk more about this "quiet time" with God, but here I want to stress going deeper with God and the steps we can take to help us do this. When we have decided that we will take time to grow in our intimacy with God, we can go on with the next step.

Step three is to find supporters who love God and also want to go deeper with God. Plan to attend a Bible study where you can learn more about God, His love, and His ways. Or perhaps meet with a friend for lunch and talk about what God is doing in your lives. The point is you need someone to encourage you to go deeper with God—someone who is on the same journey as you, that is, to further your spiritual relationship with Christ.

The following step is to evaluate where you are in your Christian commitment. Are you complacent, nominal or on fire for more of God? Again, I say to pray for God to light that fire of desire inside you—only He can do it. Don't sit on the fence but decide you will follow God with all your heart.

The last step is to face yourself and to face what might be standing in the way of your intimacy with Christ. Perhaps it is some sin, bitterness, anger, pride, etc. I know that one of the reasons that I might be ignoring God is because of laziness, lack of discipline, and selfishness. Sometimes, I would rather watch a movie, or talk on the phone than to meet with God. Ask the Lord to show you anything that may be blocking your intimacy with Him, and He will reveal it to you. Then, ask Him for the strength to do what He is asking you to do in order to be free to grow deep roots in Him.

Go deeper with God and hide in Him for He will keep you safe and keep you under His sheltering wing. Allow Him to love you—receive His love and invite a romance between you both. He is ready and waiting.

<u>Discussion Questions:</u>

1. Write out mindset # Four.
2. For us to survive through our suffering, what must we do?
3. Why must we learn His Word, especially at this season?
4. Write down one of your own favorite Scriptures that has encouraged you in the Lord.
5. What are five ways we can go deeper with God?

<u>Bible Study</u>

1. In Ephesians 6:17, how do we arm our minds and what do we use as our weapon against the things Satan throws at us?
2. The helmet of Salvation is the mindset that we are in Christ, secure, forgiven and sealed. We use the Word of God to refute Satan's lies.
3. In 2 Corinthians 10:4-5, how do we demolish arguments in our minds that are opposite of the Word of God?
4. How are we empowered to do this?
5. What does James 4:8a say for us to do? What will God do?

Mindset Number Five: *What we are thinking about produces how we feel and influences how we will act.*

It is vitally important to monitor our thinking so we can take control of our lives. What we think about has a direct influence on how we will feel and behave. When we are entertaining thoughts about losing control, not being able to stand the stress, or continuing struggles, this sets off the chemicals in our body and brain to respond to those messages.

In my own life, I know this to be absolutely true. I have thoughts of fear swirling around in my head and that sets off panic in my body, thus making me feel like I am losing control. So, I start acting like I am out of control and thus on goes the pattern. I realize that sometimes it is very difficult to grasp what we are thinking about and to change it because our feelings are so strongly connected to our thinking. We may feel like one big tidal wave of emotions going wild; but even though our emotions may seem to be the thing that is in control, at the moment, they need not be.

You see, when our emotions are raving and storming, we can still set our *will* and *choose* to take this or that action—something that will be healthy and positive for us; we can choose to change our focus even if our thoughts are raging lies. If we stay steady, eventually our emotions will have to line up with the truths that we choose to tell ourselves and we can experience some peace and confidence.

I do this all the time. Because of my illness of OCD, also called "the doubting disease," I cannot rely on my emotions; I have to set my will to make the right choices for what I will think and do. I have found this works time and time again. Don't forget that exercising our will to choose to think on what pleases God and building ourselves up, and encouraging ourselves, is a process. It takes self-control and patience, and God wants to develop this fruit of the Spirit in our hearts and lives—He wants to teach us self-control and patience empowered by the Holy Spirit. Remember, our emotions and feelings may seem very strong and clamor for all our attention; however, don't be deceived--you don't have to live as a slave to your emotions. You can find victory in your emotional life by choosing to refute the lies with the truth and holding fast to what is good.

So, when we are feeling panicky we must listen to what we are saying to ourselves. Are we listening to some misbeliefs? Then, we must change what we are thinking and put on a right mindset. Grab a Scripture and focus in on it to jolt your thinking out of the negative pattern it is in; start to praise God in song or pray for someone aloud. If you are in a public place, try to get to a restroom where there will be more privacy; or have some Scriptures written out on cards in your purse that you can pull out in time of need. Find what works for you so that your feelings and emotions won't get the upper hand. Remember that what you are feeling is just that, a feeling, a mood of the moment and it will change. Then pray; always pray.

Discussion Questions:

1. Write out our last mindset #Five.
2. Write out an inventory of what you have been telling yourself lately.
3. Refute any lies with the truth.
    Example: <u>Lie: I feel hopeless</u>
    <u>Refute with truth:</u> Even though I may feel hopeless God is with me and He will give me the strength I need to make it through. These are just feelings of the moment and they will not last.

Now I'll conclude this part on "mindset" with some encouraging words for discouraging moments. Keep these for reference whenever you feel down and need a little lift.

∞

When lonely:

> *Did you know you are not alone in your painful moment? Someone is always with you. That someone is God.*

∞

> *You're going to make it!*

> *Did you know that what you are feeling right now has been felt by other human beings, so again, don't be fooled into thinking your experiencing something that is so awful that you won't ever make it through.*

> *God says He'll always give us a healthy way to make it through our problems. You can count on it.*

∞

For Relief:

> *Same old painful thinking? I know, I've been there for sure. Just want to tell you if you keep hanging in there, relief will, without a doubt, finally come.*

∞

Do what the Bible says.

Do you feel like all your worst fears and problems are forcing their way into and bombarding your poor tired brain, take five. Tell everything to wait. Sit down and have something good to eat or drink, like a piece of chocolate or a bunch of juicy grapes, hot cocoa, or a donut. Take three deep breaths, let them out and then slowly recite the Bible verse that says to "Cast all that is threatening to overwhelm you upon the great shoulders of the awesome King and Problem Solver, Jesus Christ (1Peter 5:7). Let His words soak into your spirit.

∞

When Worried:

Help! I can't concentrate on anything anymore but my problems. I go for a walk, they walk with me. I go for a bike ride, they are peddling along-- I sit down to eat and they seem to be expanding within my stomach as I chew in silence.

I know, I'll take a shower, and they can't stay with me there. Not when I've washed them down the drain. Enough for today. I'll take no thought for tomorrow. I've worried enough for today--time to rest my mind. I give myself permission.

∞

ROXANNE EILERS

Positive Thinking:

Remember your peace is found in Christ, so ask Him to center your heart and thoughts to where they become sound and rational.

∞

It's sunshine-bright outside, but I feel I have shades on. No matter how wide I open my eyes, I can't make them see clearer. Perhaps it's my brain. It is my brain. It's foggy today and confused and under the weather.

Nothing looks good or feels good. There come those old foreboding thoughts. They are the same ones—the ones that, if I allow them, can debilitate me, and cause me extreme emotional stress. I cannot afford to give them power over me. Not for a second. In my weakened, depressed state they come to oppress me, to shake my foundation. What will I do? Use tools I've learned.

To the best of my ability I will talk myself through. To the best of my ability I will let Jesus Christ guide me through each difficult moment. I will look for the glimpses of hope, and I will do something good that will bring some relief to my nervous body and dark cloudy mind.

I'll tell myself I don't need to figure it all out this very moment. I'll tell myself God has all the answers, so I will hold fast to the faith I do have and let God have my worries. Then I will tell myself I will feel better and I will have a better day, because I have been here before, and God has been here before with me. He is faithful.

∞

Changing Days and Seasons:

Feelings fluctuate and change. I may feel very uncomfortable, but it is just the mood of the moment. I know this because I have been here before. I remember when my sister died. Feelings and moods were the change of the day. Well, it's the same with the feelings of depression. Feelings come and go; they can change from one moment to the next.

I need to focus on reality and my now. Not on what was or what will be, or can be, but what is. Before I know it, these days and moments that hurt so bad will be as a hazy memory as when a woman gives birth to her baby; the memory of the labor and delivery pain will fade with time.
A few good days can put to flight many bad ones.

Only God can place purpose in my heart. He can change the apathy, the listlessness, the hopeless feeling—to zest for life, adventure to grow, and a clear eye of excelling growing faith and hope.

Seems like this dark time has lasted for weeks. But it just takes that one morning when everything changes and life looks good and promising again. And it will come.

ROXANNE EILERS

∞

Sufficient Grace:

I am so afraid of what lies before me--I can't do this. I will fail or make a terrible mistake.

Okay, I can allow myself to be stuck in this way of thinking or I can tell myself that "I can do whatever I need to do through Christ's power that strengthens me." And I don't have to face tomorrow, today. I will have plenty of grace for whatever I must face in the coming days, weeks, and years. Then, if I happen to make a mistake or fail at something, I won't be demolished; I can face myself and whatever consequences that may follow. Mistakes happen. I won't die.

∞

Panic! Help now!

I'm feeling awfully panicky right now--it feels terrible--I can't stand it! What if I go crazy or do something terrible; what if I have a heart attack, or can't breathe? What if I die?

I can stand feelings of panic, and that is all it is--a feeling of panic. My body reacts to what I have been thinking about so I will change my thoughts. This panic will not overwhelm me. It will not dictate how I will live; in fact, I will get my mind refocused on something healthy--like reading a good book, watching a fun movie, going for a brisk walk, talking to God in prayer, making myself laugh at myself. I won't go crazy, because God has given me a sound mind. I won't go crazy because I won't allow myself to.

Most people who have panic attacks never have heart attacks--or die for lack of oxygen.

∞

Higher Gain:

I can't stand one more thing! Everything has gone wrong for me. I feel hopeless and worn out. I can't go through this again.

Somehow, Jesus experienced everything I am going through right now, in some way--He can relate to me. He had to face excruciating suffering, loss, betrayal, and then the horrific death of being crucified. I want to do what He did when facing all of these things. I want to focus in on tolerating my suffering and discomfort for a higher gain. Jesus' higher gain was to see us redeemed and walking with Him in fellowship. My higher gain is to see my problem solved, to make it through these days so that I can help others, to see a life changed, to be healthy emotionally, to be all that God has planned for me to be.

∞

ROXANNE EILERS

Financial Problems:

How will I pay the rent this month? How will I afford groceries? I have no job. I've been sick. The money has run out. Where do I turn?

I know that God has promised to take care of me. If I trust Him He will show Himself to me in a powerful way. He has taken care of me in the past-- He will provide for me in the present. So, I will look to Him and take my worries to Him in prayer. He will answer me because He said He would. I will make it through this lean time. I will have compassion on others who also go through these kinds of trials.

∞

Death:

I'm worried about dying. I don't want to die. I don't want my loved ones to die. I am so afraid I won't make it emotionally if I lose a loved one. I will be left alone. What if I lose my parents, a spouse, a child, or a sibling--it will hurt too much, I won't be able to stand it? What if they aren't saved when they die?

I'm hugging myself right now and calming my heart down. Now I will talk to myself the way Jesus wants me to--in faith and hope. First of all, I don't have dying grace right now because I don't need it. I have living grace--I need that! Second, we all will die someday; this is just part of life. . .and it's okay. Jesus tasted death for all of us, so He will be with us when it is our turn to leave this world.

Yes, my loved ones will also one day die, but I know I will make it emotionally because God will give me the strength and grace I will need at that time. He has before and He will then. I am never alone even if I lose a loved one. The Great Comforter is always with me. I also have people who love me. I can stand whatever I must in this life. Others have gone through losses and I will be able to also.

God knows I want my whole family saved and I believe He will answer my prayers. It is not His will that any should perish but that all come to repentance. So, I am praying for His will to be done.

∞

Care Giver:

This is too hard, taking care of this person. I am so weary and tired. She is so demanding and I constantly feel irritated by her. Lord, take away this burden.
I can hear Jesus saying to me, "Give care out of love for Me, child. This season will soon be over and the lessons you are learning are of great value. Learn the lessons well for there is always a purpose in everything. I will assist you in your work. Come to Me and I will give you the rest and

refreshing you need. Show My love--be My hands, be My heart to this dear one. Knowing these things will sustain you until your season is up." And I was sustained!

∞

Unwanted Thoughts:

When thoughts come into my mind that deeply trouble me, or cause me fear and great anxiety I don't have to let them stay. . .just like birds can fly over my head, but I don't need to let them make nests in my hair.

∞

Feeling Capable:

I don't feel I can do what You have asked me to do, Lord. I don't feel capable--I doubt myself and my abilities.

But I know that You would not have asked me to do something I could not do. You promised to give me the strength to accomplish what You sent me out to do. You have prepared assignments for me and my particular personality and temperament--things designed just for me to do. No one can do them like me. You will be with me and I will do my best; my best will be good enough and I will give You glory.

∞

Nuclear War:

Lord, what will I do if there is a nuclear war and I have nowhere to hide, and it's headed my way? This thought terrifies me.

I can hear Your answer. It is always the same. Don't worry about tomorrow; there will be wars and rumors of wars but the end is not yet. I am even in control of war. You will have whatever grace you need for whatever you must face. Live in the present and grow in knowing and loving Me.

ROXANNE EILERS

3) Have Encouraging Hand-Holders

In order to make it through hard times we desperately need people who will give us a word of encouragement and a hand of support. In her book, *Balcony People*, Joyce Landorf Heatherley talks about balcony people who cheer us on from the balcony. They are people that find the good in you and encourage you (Landorf Heatherley 1989). I found that when I am truly feeling overwhelmed in a trial, it is crucial to have some balcony people, some close Christian friends to love and support me. I believe when someone holds us up in prayer, listens to our heart's cry, and surrounds us with love and care, sympathy and understanding, plus truth, they help us carry our burdens. God made it to work like that.

One time when Ike and I were struggling financially while we were in school, we had to move from our apartment because we couldn't pay the rent. We didn't know where we would go and we were in desperate need for money. To our surprise, two classmates of ours not only supported us emotionally but also with financial gifts! How precious it was to our hearts. God uses the Body of Christ to minister to each other, to build each other up in our time of need.

I remember another time when my sister passed away from breast cancer, and I was in a state of grieving. This was the first time I had lost a loved one so close to me, and I really needed emotional support. God knew this and had already planned a place for me where I would be able to heal and recover. God set me, by His own hand, in the middle of a Bible study about the *Sufferings of Job*. He plopped me right there amidst other women in a small group who were hurting and struggling also. All of us together brought healing to one another as we studied about Job's life, as we talked and shared our feelings with one another, and as we prayed. I felt I was not alone. Through prayer and Bible study, fellowship and fun, my sorrow and pain began to ease.

Balcony people are also those people who tell you that you can make it no matter how hard things are. They believe in you and tell you so. These people are there when you need them, and find joy in being an encouragement. When I think of my friends, I realize that I have been blessed by so many people who believe in me and in what I can do. I love them and appreciate them immensely.

Included with these balcony people are those who have years of godly wisdom under their belts. They can give us wise counsel when we need it, and boy, do we need wise counsel in times of trial. Sometimes, it is so easy to get wrapped up in what we are feeling and going through, we cannot see the big picture at all. We need someone to give us a reality check. We need people with a balanced perspective who can see what we are going through --who have a clearer perspective than ours.

Remember: Iron sharpens iron, as one friend to another, and we must be teachable instead of prideful and defensive (Proverbs 27:17).

ROXANNE EILERS

So often when we are suffering and depressed we do not want anyone to bother us. We become defensive and feel like we need to pretend that everything is okay. Can we be what we are? Just human beings? Can we allow ourselves to be transparent so others can comfort us? Pride often prevents us from receiving all that God wants to do for us through the Body of Christ. God does not want us to stay away from others, but to be part of the family of God, sharing our wounds and pain in a safe atmosphere, with safe people, and where there is safe confidentiality.

One of the worst things that we can do is to hide ourselves away when we are hurting and life seems so perplexing. One of the best things we can do is to allow our hearts to connect with God's people because they can be used as His hands, feet, mouth, and heart to bring encouragement to us. Say "yes" to love when it presents itself even if it's just a smile. Say "yes" when love wants to serve you in some way. This is pleasing to the Lord.

Yes, God wants us to build each other up, for this is how He is, always encouraging us in our walk with Him. In the New Testament of the Bible, we see Paul the apostle exhorting the Thessalonian Christians to "encourage one another and to continue to build each other up" as they had already been doing (1 Thess. 5:11). Talk about suffering, this church was going through terrible persecutions and fiery trials, yet during it all they were balcony people encouraging those who were also going through sufferings.

Taking a look at that word "encourage" we will see that this word is actually the Greek word, *parakaleo*. This word can be found translated differently throughout the New Testament. Some of these translations are: "to exhort, to admonish, to teach, to entreat or beseech, to console, to encourage and to comfort." That's quite a bit of nourishment from that one word isn't it (Getz 1972)?

To summarize, we are to share the truth with each other in love (Eph.4:15)—that is by exhortation, teaching and admonishing. When we are near-sighted and have lost perspective of our suffering and pain, it is our encouragers who can tell us what is reality, and they can help us to see the larger and healthier picture. When we falter and waver in our faith, it is our encouragers who will entreat and beseech us to keep the faith and strengthen us. Finally, we are not only to receive for ourselves this care from our encouragers or balcony people, but we too are called to console, encourage and comfort others—become balcony people ourselves. This means we don't tear down or criticize. This means we are to tenderly deal with each other in love and concern.

<u>Discussion Questions:</u>

4. Who do we need besides the Lord in times of suffering?
5. What positive things can we learn and receive from others?
6. What is one of the worst things we can do when we are hurting?
7. What is one of the best things we can do?

ROXANNE EILERS

<u>Bible Study</u>

1. Read 1 Corinthians 12:12-14, briefly summarize these verses about the Body of Christ.
2. In Ephesians 4:15-16, who is the Head and how is the Body of Christ joined and held together?
3. How does this apply to you?
4. In Acts 14:21-22, what do we find Paul and Barnabas doing for the other believers? So what are we to do with one another? Who will God use?
5. Then in Proverbs 27:17, what do you think "sharpen" means?

4) Pray Always In Everything.

One of the greatest tools and weapons we can use during suffering is prayer. When I am suffering, you *will* find me praying. I pray about everything that concerns me and worries me, whether big or small. I ask God to relax my nervous stomach, to quiet my brainwaves, to intervene in a loved one's life who is in crisis, to help me find the right dress—anything that concerns me will find itself in a prayer. I pray morning, noon, and night . . .I am ready to pray at any time. Praying helps bring order and calmness to my every situation.

In David Ray's book, *The Art of Christian Meditation*, he says that prayer is spiritual communication with God; it is intimately participating in conversation with the "Almighty." The purpose of us relying on prayer is to draw us one step at a time in becoming aware of the presence of God and who He is (Ray 1977). We are also brought into a deeper knowledge and understanding of what our purpose in life is to be. Prayer is a crucial part of being able to hold on to hope in a time of need. In fact, without it we will wither up and die in our spiritual life and walk. Prayer, to our spirit, is as vital as oxygen to our lungs. We know Jesus prayed and I will be touching on His model of prayer in the following paragraphs.

In his book, *In the Name of Jesus*, Henri Nouwen talks about the discipline of prayer as being a strategy that can protect us from the world's pull, and he speaks how important it is to pray about what issues tug at our hearts. Prayer keeps us in an intimate relationship with God; we come to know His heart and our own heart better (Nouwen 1989). We will be looking at our intimate time with God, but here, my focus will be on prayer and some of the models of prayer and types of prayer that can help us cultivate our own life of prayer.

There are different ways of practicing prayer and I would like to share some ways that I think can be very beneficial. The first one I'd like to address is the model of the "Our Father" which is found in Matt. 6:9-13.

> *Our Father in heaven, hallowed be Your name, Your kingdom come, Your will be done, on earth as it is in heaven. Give us today our daily bread. And forgive us our debts, as we also have forgiven our debtors. And lead us not into temptation, but deliver us from the evil one. For Yours is the kingdom and the power and the glory forever. Amen.*

The Lord Jesus takes His disciples through the steps of basic prayer. First, we are to petition God that His name be lifted up in heaven and on earth, that all men may bring glory to the name of Jesus. We may pray that the Lord will bring glory to Himself out of our suffering. We are to praise Him always, not for the bad, but for how He is going to turn it into something that will bring Him glory. We may feel that everything is against us, but God knows what is really happening.

Thus, we give glory to the Father. We begin with praise and glorification of the name of God.

Next, we ask that God's kingdom continue to make its way into our lives, the lives of those around us, and finally be completely ushered in at the end of the Age when Christ comes back again to earth. We pray that God's will be done on earth just as it is always done in heaven. May God's will be done in our own lives, in our own characters, in our own hearts and minds. May God's will be done in our circumstances, and may He have His way in the midst of our suffering. Remember, we may use this basic prayer model by personalizing it. We can pray that God would use us to fulfill His will.

Then, we are to ask for what we need for this day--for our daily needs, spiritually, emotionally, and physically. This is so wonderful because we can take everything that is concerning us to God and know that He will do something about it. From the smallest concern like an aching foot to a serious concern like a sick child. Whatever we need, we can go to our good Father in heaven who hears us. Thank you, Lord!

The next step is that we ask for forgiveness for our sins and short comings, and at the same time ask God to reveal to us anyone we personally have not forgiven. We are requested, then, to forgive those people. By an act of our will we can choose to forgive; we do not need to wait until we feel something. God will work with our will and our emotions--He will help us.

Following this time of forgiveness, we are to petition that we would not be placed in a position to be tested or tempted, and that God Himself would deliver us from evil and the Evil One. We can pray for deliverance from trials and temptations. If we are in a trying period, we can ask God to deliver us out of it according to His will. David prays for deliverance all through the Psalms and he attests that God hears, or will hear him. God then does something about it--He delivers David.

Finally, the prayer ends with giving glory once more to God. We open with praise and end with praise. "For Yours is the kingdom, and the power and the glory forever. Amen."
The next model of prayer is called the "Consciousness Examen" compiled by George A. Aschenbrenner (Aschenbrenner1972). I learned this model when I was working on my MTS in my leadership class. The "Consciousness Examen" method has five steps:

1) First, we quiet ourselves and ask the Holy Spirit where in our lives we have shut God out or opened up to Him.
2) We thank God for His blessings of that moment.
3) We check and reflect on where our heart is in terms of its spirituality. Have we sought God and a greater intimacy with Him? Where has He been present? This is called "consolation." "Desolation" is seeking where in our life God has been seemingly absent. Did we resist His voice?

4) Then, we acknowledge and confess our short comings and receive grace to accept forgiveness.

5) Finally, we make changes and show repentant behavior--"resolution."

These steps are easy to follow, but take a little time--you don't want to be in a hurry. The Examen is used to help us gauge where we are spiritually. We learn to move closer to those actions that are godly and less selfish. Because we are examining ourselves, where we need to grow spiritually, we can make choices to be more open to God—more open to the changes He is asking us to make in order to be transformed into the image of Christ. This is a good model to use when we are having our quiet time with God, before we read His Word.

Prayer can be a divine therapy in our lives. God has done much therapy on my heart and mind during my times of prayer with Him. Repentance takes place first, a cleansing, then I can hear God speaking to me more clearly, and I can respond to what He brings before me from my subconscious into my consciousness. I can experience an inner rest the more I become sensitive to God's gracious and healing presence.

When an emotional wound surfaces, we can take it to God and receive His love and acceptance, this will gradually bring inner healing and consequently bring us one step closer to experiencing emotional and spiritual wholeness (Thomas Keating 2012). It is important that we make God the center point of our lives so that transformation can occur. God can transform our thinking and attitudes as we sit in His presence; He can bring healing to our battered and weary spirit and mind. Friend, this is the learning part of how to hold on to hope in your season of suffering-- knowing how to pray. So many things happen during our prayer time. It is a good idea to keep a journal so that you can see what God is doing in your life, and in what direction He is leading you so you can learn the heart of God and His wisdom.

There is also another model where we pray the Scriptures. This model is one of the purest forms of prayer to God. The Word of God opens our hearts to a simple and genuine faith because God's Word is inspired by the Holy Spirit and it is living and powerful. Somehow the Word of God penetrates our hearts and thoughts as we pray God's heart back to Him and this strengthens our faith. Praying the Scriptures also teaches us how and what to pray for. An example of this would be in Mark 14:38 where Jesus tells us to "Watch and pray, lest you enter into temptation." The Bible instructs us to watch and pray so that we will not be sluggish in our resisting of temptation. In praying this Scripture back to God we would pray: "Lord, please help me to watch and pray so that I won't enter into temptation." Or, "Lord, I am watching and praying so that I won't enter into temptation."

Another example could be found in Psalm 66:17 and 19-20. "I cried to Him with my mouth, and He was extolled with my tongue. . .Certainly God has heard me; He has attended to the voice of my prayer.

Blessed be God, who has not turned away my prayer, nor His mercy from me!" God wants us to cry out to Him audibly and to worship Him in faith. He wants us to believe that He has heard us, that He has drawn near, and that He has already answered our prayer. In praying this Psalm back to the Lord, you may want to say, "I cry to You with my mouth, and extol You with my tongue, O Lord! I praise You for You have heard my cry and have attended to my prayer. I bless You, O Lord because You have not turned away my prayer about (mention what your need is, or the need of someone else) and Your mercy has been poured out on me!"

This is a beautiful way to pray and I have practiced and continue to use this method. As we pray the Scriptures we become intimately involved with the Father, Son and Holy Spirit. It is said that when we pray the Scriptures we are doing something that is "practical and productive." Not only is it effective now in the present, but also throughout eternity. We blend our prayers with the Word of God, and Jesus, our wonderful intercessor, brings our requests before the throne of the Father (Judson Cornwall 1990).

Finally, a model I call my own is "The Prayer of the Moment." When I was going through seasons of extreme suffering I found it was hard to even pray because I was so exhausted from battling compulsive thoughts in my mind. To be able to pray at all, I would pray with all my heart for whatever the need was right at that very moment. I would cry out to God with simple words and a simple plea—just like a child. I would lift my voice to Him, and He would hear and comfort me. Most of the time, as soon as I prayed, the answer would come to me through a Scripture or a thought from God.

There are times when all we can do is to sit silently in God's presence. These are the times we are so worn and weary that no words will even come to our lips. But God knows our hearts at these times and just loves us--He holds us close to His heart and sings His song over us.

Write out a prayer to the Lord about what is on your heart right now.

Types of Prayer

There are different types of prayer. I will not be addressing all of them, but I will touch on a few. It is best to get a book on prayer as there are so many good ones out now. Included in a discussion of types of prayer are: the prayer of agreement, petition, intercession, worship, and prayer of authority over Satan.

The prayer of agreement is done with other believers. It is a powerful way to pray. Jesus says, "Again, truly, I tell you that if two of you on earth agree about anything they ask for, it will be done for them by My Father in heaven. For where two or three gather in My name, there am I with them" (Matthew 18:19-20). When we stand together about a matter, and agree on what we are praying about God will answer-- He says He will. When we call on God with like minds and faith, our prayers are powerful and they will work. The prayer of a righteous man is powerful and it works (James 5:16b)! These kinds of prayer will bring results as they penetrate heaven.

In the prayer of petition we can pour out our hearts before God. We can intimately hear from God what steps we are to take next, or what to do in a certain situation. God wants us to take everything to Him in prayer—all our petitions, everything on our hearts. We can cry out to Him as our dear Father in heaven who listens intently to our voice in prayer. Nothing is too small that we can't take it before the throne of our Daddy. The Bible tells us in Hebrews 4: 16 to come before His "throne of grace with confidence, so that we may receive mercy and find grace to help us in our time of need."

In intercession, we can pray for others who are hurting or in need. We can stand in the gap for them before God. **Remember: In praying for others we get our minds off ourselves, and on to God things.** So often, in my times of trial, God has asked me to pray for particular people. Even though it is difficult to turn our minds away from our own pain and focus our attention on the needs of others, this is a necessity if we are to keep holding on to our hope. God blesses the time that we spend in prayer for others; this pleases Him. If you sense that God is tugging at your heart to intercede for someone, stop at once and pray. You never know, you may help save someone's life, or bring deliverance to a person in great bondage. Obey the Holy Spirit as He nudges your spirit and you will be blessed.

Worship and praise are other forms of prayer we can lift up to the Lord. We turn our focus upon God and away from our problems and sufferings. As we place our focus on God, who He is and what He has already accomplished in the past, our faith and hope are magnified. Be sure to give God thanks for all He has done and is going to do. Something supernatural takes place when we adore God. He comes down and reveals Himself to us intimately. What happens inside our hearts? A work takes place in our hearts, and our faith is encouraged; thus, we are ready for a second round of fight. Worship and praise turn our eyes upon Jesus. It can help bring our lives into a proper perspective. We will be able to see the situation more clearly; we will be able to get a glimpse of the truth that we do not have to be defeated nor swallowed up by our trials, but God will do for us what He has purposed. He is indeed in control.

God also gives us the authority in prayer to speak out in faith to bind and rebuke the devil and to break his power that holds people in bondage. Sometimes, we need to have a strong Christian believer pray over us and break any holds the devil has trapped us in. In faith, they can help us tear down the strongholds that have been oppressing our minds. We never have to be afraid of the enemy, for Jesus told us in Luke 10:18-19: "I saw Satan fall like lightning from heaven. I have given you authority to trample on snakes and scorpions and to overcome all the power of the enemy; nothing will harm you."

Jesus prayed when He was under great suffering, He also quoted and stood upon the Scriptures, while rebuking Satan and his foes (Luke 4:1-13). We can say, "In the Name of Jesus Christ, I command you, Satan to leave at once." Or perhaps we need to say, "Come out of him now! In Jesus' Mighty Name." As we draw near to the Lord He will empower us to stand against the wiles of the devil, and show us how to pray. There are wonderful books on prayer written by author Stormie Omartian that would be a great blessing to those who want to grow in their prayer lives. I encourage you to consider them.

<u>Discussion Questions:</u>

1. What does God want us to pray about?
2. List the five kinds of prayer and a comment about them.

<u>Bible Study</u>

1. What does Luke 6:12 tell us about Jesus?
2. Colossians 4:2 tells us we are to do something. What are we to do in this verse?
3. Summarize Philippians 4:6 in a sentence or two.
4. In Ephesians 6:18 what part of the Armor of God are we to use against the enemy?
5. I love the verses in James 5:16-18. What are the elders of the church to do for us?
6. What does the Bible say about our relationship to other believers?
7. Because we are made righteous in Christ our prayers become powerful and effective. If your Bible translation uses the word "effective "or something similar, what does this mean to you?
8. According to Hebrews 13:15 and Psalm 106:1, what do these verses say about praise and thanksgiving?

Finally, I have written out some prayers you may want to pray at certain times, all prayed in the name of Jesus Christ.

Guidance: Dear Father, I ask for Your divine guidance in my life right this minute and in the days to follow. Please guide me with Your eye and place Your hand upon me. Direct my thoughts to where they are glorifying to You. Direct my thoughts in the way You would have me go. Please touch my spirit and help me to hear Your voice clearly. Place me just where You want me to be. *In Jesus Name, I pray, Amen.*

Emotional and physical strength: Dear Father, touch my total life. How I need Your strength right this moment. My brain is full of worry and fear, my body feels like it is drained of strength. Infuse Your divine God life into me. Breathe into me and awaken my sluggish mind and heart-- awaken my weak flesh so I may serve You with all my heart and all my might, and my entire mind.

Provision: Dear Father, I am in need today. I come to You because You said You will supply my need according to Your riches in glory by Christ Jesus. My need today is___________and so I lay it before You and I ask You to supply everything for this need that is required. Thank You Dear Father, I believe that this need is being met right now, and so I rest in Your great provision.

Healing: Dear Father, according to what Jesus did on the cross, according to the stripes that were laid upon His back, according to Your mercy and goodness, according to Your power and might, restore me. Heal me and make me whole, and bring Yourself glory and honor. Today, I ask You to send forth Your divine health into my body, my mind, my brain, my spirit, into all my organs, muscles, bones, into every single cell. Remove what is diseased and bring wholeness to my life.

Spiritual renewal: Dear Father, I thirst, not for the water of this life, but for Your living water to fill me up. Wash away my sins, fears, guilt, and wanderings. Drench me in Your Spirit till I am ready to burst out of a new wine skin and water all of those who are spiritually thirsty and parched. Pour out Your Holy Spirit into every area of my life and renew me, revive me, restore me.

Grace for Suffering: Dear Father, I don't like this suffering. It hurts! Oh Refiner, Thou who sits at the fire, refine me, refine me and more, but in the fire soothe my pain. Give me great grace for suffering according to Your will. Surround me with mercies and graces divine. Let me dance with You in the flame, in the water, in the valley. Let me see Your face and feel Your presence. I know I can make it with one touch from Your hand. Show me the way through, under and over, so I can be able to bear up under this trouble. But Lord, even if you seem silent, though You slay me, yet will I trust You, because no suffering is forever, but the fruits of righteousness will remain. Give me a glimpse of hope; help me to find the treasures of darkness in my suffering. Enable me to stand!

Salvation for a Loved One: Dear Father, You said You are not willing that any should perish but that all would come to repentance. You so loved the world that You gave Your only begotten Son that whosoever believes in Him will not perish but have everlasting life. It is Your will that my loved ones receive Your great, excellent salvation and it is not Your will that they perish. So, I pray in faith, believing that You will save_________. Do what You must do in their lives so that they will come to You. I break the power of Satan from their lives, in Jesus' Name, so that they may see the light and come to You. Now I claim their inheritance and salvation for You, Amen and Amen.

Hearing God's Voice: Dear Father, I want to hear You. Speak to me Lord, I am listening. Open my spiritual eyes so I can see what You are showing me this moment. Draw my heart away from the things that are crowding it and reveal to me Your glory, Your Word, Yourself. In Jesus Name I pray, Amen.

Discussion Question: From the example prayers which was your favorite and why?

ROXANNE EILERS

5) Let God Develop and Use You.

When God is molding us into His image, at times it really hurts, doesn't it? The fires of suffering are burning away the dross from our lives and purifying us. I found that in my time of trial when I look for opportunities to bless others around me, or those whom God brings into my path, my life is enriched and my suffering is somewhat eased. Sometimes this would mean pulling out of my being, gaining enough strength to make that little card for someone who needs a lift. It really blesses me to give in this way out of my creative ministry. I find it complete joy!

Remember, even in our own pain, as we enter the pain of another, our pain can be somewhat eased.

We are allowing God to love through us even while we are hurting—wow! Does this build godly character! It is when we are nearsighted with self-pity, and absorbed in our own woes that we can really feel the fires of trial become so hot that we think we will be burned up and consumed. The devil would love to have us become paralyzed spiritually and emotionally by our situation through fear and panic. Then, we are of no blessing to others. God must further purify our hearts and teach us to turn our eyes to Him.

As we are suffering, God does not forget about the gifts He's bestowed upon us. He wants us to use our gifts to bring encouragement to others. To use our gifts to bring glory to God, it is vital that we come humbly before the One who gave us the gifts. Then, we need to ask Him what He wants us to do, where He wants us to go, and to whom He wants us to serve with our gifts. We are born with gifts that God has already placed within us just waiting to be developed. The more we exercise our gifts the more effective they become.

<u>Seven Ministry Gifts</u>

There are seven ministry gifts that I would like to touch on; perhaps you will see yourself in one or more of these gifts. The first three are: ministering, teaching and exhorting. Ministering denotes "serving the needs of others" to those in the church and those outside the church. This is a ministry that takes interest in meeting the practical needs of people. For instance, a person with the gift of ministering will see a need and want to help fill it. Perhaps the need comes from someone who doesn't have a ride to church, hospital or to the grocery store. Maybe someone has the need for finances; they can't pay the rent. The person with the gift of ministering sees these needs and has the desire to meet them. It is a joy for them to help others.

The teacher, on the other hand, shows people how to do things; they educate and train others. Any person in the church body can have this gift, but it is different than the pastor-teacher who is in a position of overseeing the church. Teaching and exhorting go hand in hand, and one of the main ingredients is to encourage people to grow, spiritually, emotionally, intellectually. A teacher/exhorter will see a gift in another person and want to help her/him to develop it so that others may be blessed. A teacher wants to impart knowledge; she/he is not always satisfied with just imparting knowledge though, but also concentrates on showing how something is done for the learner to be able to perform it himself. I am a teacher and I fully enjoy using this gift as God opens the door; it is my main gift. I can't wait to impart knowledge and application of spiritual things in the lives of those whom God brings to my attention.

The last four ministry gifts are: giving, ruling, showing mercy and helping. With the gift of giving, I think we all understand what the gift of giving implies. It occurs when people want to give from their hearts liberally. They want to give of their finances, time, abilities, resources and so forth. In 2 Corinthians 9:7 we are told to give from the heart because God loves a giver who has a cheerful attitude about their giving.

As we look at the gift of ruling, we will see that this has to do with directing or governing. Rulers are people who lead the Body of Christ and "preside" over them and direct them. They normally find themselves organizing and managing affairs and people. Organizing luncheons, Bible studies, and special get-togethers with friends, thinking of others in these ways is part of being a ruler. Managing and administrating are what a ruler does best. He/she respects authority and works within the confines of true authority, and knows how to facilitate resources. A ruler is also a visionary and sees what can be created for the future; he/she works towards that end enjoying thoroughly his/her work. These people are natural leaders (Fortune 1987).

Hope In A Season Of Suffering

The gift of showing mercy or compassion is being able to "feel with or for another." Jesus had compassion (mercy) on the crowds when He saw them. He saw them as "sheep without a shepherd" (Matt. 9:36). Often the gospels state that Jesus was "moved with pity" as He healed the people. When we have mercy towards someone we are moved to do something to ease their pain. The gift of mercy or compassion is directly related to those in discomfort and pain. How beautiful Jesus was when He was moved to perform a miracle for someone who was ignored or treated unkindly by others. When we see a person who is hurting in some way and we feel a tugging in our spirit toward compassion, this is the gift of mercy, so show mercy. Pray with someone, or give someone a hug or just be there for them.

The gift of helps deals with helping people by doing deeds of goodness. The Holy Spirit empowers these people to share this gift and they enjoy helping and assisting others. They can assist leaders in the church, and they can help get work accomplished in different areas to further the kingdom. Praying comes under helps, as does visiting the sick and the elderly, cooking meals for someone who is sick, et cetera (Brandt 1978).

In their book, *Discover Your God-Given Gifts*, Don and Katie Fortune give detailed characteristics and uses of our God-given gifts. This book is an excellent tool for further study on this subject. The authors mention at the end of their book different possible areas of ministry. These are: "Prayer and healing, practical ministries, educational ministries, counseling ministries, outreach ministries, leadership ministries, caring ministries, and creative ministries" (Fortune 1987). Do any of these gifts ring a bell in your heart? That is the Holy Spirit confirming your gift to you. Do a study on the gifts and enjoy learning more about your gifting; you will also be able to see these gifts in other people's lives and you can further encourage them to use their gifts. Think of what you can do—the more you develop and use your gifts, the more aware and better skilled you become; you also will be more sensitive to learning the voice and guidance of the Holy Spirit as He leads you to use these gifts.

So, send a card, or a special book to someone; if you can sing, sing as opportunities open—even if you don't feel like it. God doesn't tell us to wait until we feel good enough to give. Give a smile, bring over a hot plate of food to one in need. Make that needed phone call, or take some flowers over, give some of your time, or give words of encouragement. Be available to be used by God even in your time of suffering. Do what you can do in your season. I realize that sometimes God just asks us to rest and wait on Him, but ask the Lord what He wants you to do, and where He wants you to serve, and in what capacity. God wired us for service and has given us gifts to use. If we take the steps to step out of ourselves, to give of ourselves, growth takes place, and our abilities are further developed. Thus, God is honored and He will supply you with the grace needed to serve.

Remember: He who blesses others will himself be blessed.

Discussion Questions:

1. What should we be looking for especially in times of struggle and hardship?
2. What would the Devil love to have us become?
3. When we choose to give of ourselves, what takes place? What happens to us?
4. What are some of your gifts?
5. How can you use them to bless others and glorify God? Brain storm here.

Bible Study

1. Read Romans 12:3-8.
2. 1 Peter 4:10-11 tells us to use our gifts to do what?

   Why? What will be the final outcome?
3. 2 Timothy 1:6 tells us to use our gifts to do what?
4. How does this apply to you today?
5. According to Proverbs 11:25, if we bless and refresh others with our gifts, what will be the outcome for us? God gives each of us gifts and the needed faith with which to use them.

6) Get Away With God.

Catherine Martin, founder of "Quiet Time Ministries," is an expert in the field of spending time with God. I have grown under her ministry and love her books. She has written several books for quiet times with the Lord. Her love for Him is evident in her books and sharing, so I have included her contact information on the page "End Notes" for those who wish to reach her. She has been one of the main mentors in my life that has encouraged me to "get away with God."

It is so necessary to spend time with the Lord by ourselves during periods of suffering. Be it ten minutes or an hour. The time we spend in His Word and intimate communication will strengthen our souls, renew our hope, and refuel us to keep going on. We must draw back to refuel, so no matter how busy we become, we must have an appointed time to meet with God. **Remember: Jesus got alone with the Father.** The Bible tells us in the Gospel of Matthew 14:23, "And when He had sent the multitudes away, He went up into a mountain apart to pray and when the evening was come, He was there alone." Jesus got away from the crowds and sought His Father alone and in solitude. We can also see from Matthew 26:38-39 that Jesus prayed when He was in deep suffering and in anguish. "Then He said to them, 'My soul is overwhelmed with sorrow to the point of death: stay here, and keep watch with Me.' Going a little farther, He fell with His face to the ground and prayed, 'My Father, if it is possible, may this cup be taken from Me.

Yet not as I will, but as You will.'" Jesus has suffered greatly and so He knows what we are feeling when we are hurting. He knows how to comfort and encourage us in our time of suffering. And if Jesus needed to spend that time in prayer to the Father, how much more do you and I? The Holy Spirit must empower us to go through our difficulties. And when we spend quiet time with God, this becomes a major way in which He can and will empower us to carry on. We will receive guidance, wisdom, peace, emotional strength and more. It becomes a daily choice for us to meet with God, our life line.

There is a place where we can find God that is called the secret place or the "secret of God's tabernacle" where we cannot be moved by trouble or trial. It is the place where we "dwell under the shadow of the Almighty." Hannah Whitall Smith says that this secret place wherein dwells the presence of God is the safest fortress to be in; it is safer than "a thousand Gibraltars." Trials will still come into our lives but they cannot disturb the soul in that secret place with God (Smith 1956). And friends, it takes faith to enter this quiet place where strength and hope can be found.

So, we enter in by faith; we meet with God by believing He is there to meet with us—we meet with God in our spirit and through our mind. Andrew Murray speaks about "practicing the presence of Christ." He refers to this practice as a person who lives in Christ—abides and stays in Christ (Payne 1989). When we abide in Christ we live in Him and Him in us, and it is a practicing of His presence that can become our daily habit in our quiet time with Him.

But, what do we do in that time with God? I focus my thoughts on His presence and person. Sometimes, a Scripture will help me focus—I can also use some of the models of prayer I discussed earlier. This is a good time to study the Word of God, journal prayers and answers to prayers, and to hear what the Lord is saying to you. You can listen to worship music, meditate on a Scripture, or just sit in God's presence enjoying Him.

Andrew Murray says that being with God and fellowshipping with Him is our number one need in our life in Christ (Murray 1897). He goes on to say that the "divine life" we have inside us comes to us directly from God, and it is only when we are communing with the Almighty and drawing from Him that our soul is strengthened. We are to take the time and be patient until we sense that God is "near us." How He longs for us to be with Him because He loves us so. And as we gaze upon the face of the One who loves us, and as we listen for His voice, we are transformed and restored (Murray 1897). "He restores my soul" (Psalm 23).

<u>Discussion Questions:</u>

1. What is vitally important during times of suffering? Explain why.
2. What happens when we spend time alone with God?
3. Who empowers and refreshes us during this time with God?

<u>Bible Study</u>

1. Continue to spend this time alone with God in Bible study and in prayer.
2. In Mark 6:45-46, what did Jesus do after He sent the multitudes away? What does this reveal about Jesus?
3. In 1 Samuel 30:6, David is greatly distressed. What does he do?
4. So, when you are distressed and suffering what can you do?
5. David's heart was one that desperately sought God; he spent lots of time alone with God. In Psalm 27:4-6 what are some of the things you can do when you get away with God?
6. When you seek God first what will He do for you in your time of trouble? What will be the outcome?
7. Notice in verse 6, that you still have your enemies or troubles around you, but where are you spiritually and emotionally?
8. Now take time to talk with the Lord and to worship Him! Hallelujah! You may want to

ROXANNE EILERS

pray some of the prayers that are described on pp. 85-91. Write in your journal what God has been saying to you during your time with Him.

7) Let God Work While You Trust, Rest, and Wait.

It is my belief that what keeps us wringing our hands in difficult times is that we cannot control the situation or the persons, and we really want to. We want to make that person see the truth; we want things to move along more quickly than they do. We try to work it out ourselves even when it is way over our heads. Dear One, if we have done all we can, we must lay it down upon the altar of God's care and trust Him to work it out.

Many times, I have prayed, "Lord, I give this problem to You and ask You to work on it while I go about my day, or as I sleep." Many times, I need to let go, over and over again, until I am really trusting. God wants us to learn to trust in His faithfulness. He is big enough to handle our cares. He knows every answer. He knows us intimately, so He knows what we need and just what to do in a matter. And if He wants us to do something more, He can and will make that known to us also.

Letting go is vital to our peace of mind. Many nights, I lie awake trying to find an answer to a very perplexing matter. I finally give up and give it over to the Lord the best I can. I ask Him to make things clear to me and to reveal His will as He works on the situation. Psalm 37 tells me to trust, to rest, and to wait for God. These are three very difficult things to do while in a suffering situation. But, this is the way we can learn perseverance and be trained to hear God speaking to us. To hear God's direction and voice we must wait upon Him until we hear from Him. Unless we find solitude and hear from God for our guidance, we may find ourselves going in all different directions, spreading ourselves thin, running around in circles, working doggedly, hurrying rapidly, yet not attending to the most important priorities (Heuser/Shawchuck). One of the most important aspects of our time with God is that we get the attention and ear of the Almighty when we pray (Murray 1983). We need to get God's attention, to sit before Him and ask Him to reveal Himself to us.

Now, let us turn our attention on trusting the Lord. "Trust in the Lord . . ." - What is trusting? Trust is having confidence in, and being sure of, someone or something. In this case, it is having complete confidence in God and being absolutely certain that what He has said is totally true and trustworthy and can be relied upon without doubt. *Oh Lord, help us to have unreserved confidence in You.*

Think about it. When we sit down for dinner we do not examine the chair to determine whether it will hold us or not. We do not examine each nail and bolt to see if it is loose in case the chair should collapse. We would be considered crazy if we hopped up every few minutes for fear the chair would give way under our weight. No, we sit down with ease, confidence, and trust that we may eat our meal in peace. Likewise, we are asked to trust God. He means for us to abandon ourselves to His care and keeping, having assurance that as a dear Father who overflows with love for His children, He will do good to and for us, keeping that which we have committed to Him.

We are to have confidence in God that He will do what He said He would in His Word. Why should we trust Him? First, I ask you, can you create a baby and give him a spirit? Can you understand exactly how the heart and brain keep us alive and how and why they cease functioning when our spirit leaves the body? Can you comprehend life and death, time, and eternity? Oh believer, God understands and comprehends all these things. God is God. The One who created all things. In the Book of *Job*, chapter 38, when Job was going through tremendous trials and didn't know why, God asks Job a simple God question. God asks, "Who is this that questions My wisdom with such ignorant words?" In a sense, God is saying, "How dare you not trust in My wisdom; why do you question Me, I am the Almighty Creator, the Beginning and the End of all things?" Then the Lord goes on to question Job. He asks him if he was there in the beginning when the foundations of the earth were formed. He continues to lay out His creative works and power before Job. How can you not trust Me? Look, behold who I am! I am your Maker! For more complete insight on God's discussions with Job read Job 38-41.

Oh my goodness! Should we not trust and place our confidence in God alone! He has the credentials to His name. You will trust your physician and carefully follow his prescriptions, but will you not trust your God and follow His prescriptions for life and breath? The Bible tells us it is better to trust in the Lord than to put our confidence in man (Psalm 118:8) and yet we willingly, easily trust another human being many times without question. They disappoint, but God promises not to disappoint. Psalm 22:5 tells us, "They cried unto You, and were delivered: they trusted in You, and were not confounded." That word *confounded* has the meaning of being ashamed or disappointed. Thus, we can have the assurance if we put our trust in God through Jesus Christ we will not be disappointed.

Perhaps you're saying, I'm trying to trust God but my emotions are up and down and so my faith fluctuates. Remember what I said earlier about our will being in control instead of our emotions? In the book, *Trusting God Even When Life Hurts*, Jerry Bridges says that we must choose to trust God. He says that he has struggled in his life with trusting God and was held captive by his emotions and feelings (as most of us are). He says that trusting relates to our will, not our emotions. It feels good when we feel confident in our trusting God, but it is our choice that makes the difference. He goes on to say that our feelings will later follow our will to believe. Since God is all-wise, sovereign, good, and loving we can trust Him with confidence. He will accomplish that which concerns us. So, in our situation, when we choose to trust and hand it over to the Lord, we must then rest and know that He is working on it.

"Rest in the Lord...."(NKJ). Let's take a look at this huge command. *Rest.* Let's look at the Hebrew meaning. It says, "to be silent, to be astonished, to stop, cease and quiet self, be or stand still, tarry, wait." Those are a lot of words for one word "rest." But in examining each word, I can clearly see God's Word come alive.

Hope In A Season Of Suffering

After we have given everything over into the care of God we are to be *quiet* and not full of turmoil or anxious thinking. We are to remember to be *astonished* at who God is and what He is about to do with what concerns us. *Stop* my friend! Stop trying to find an answer, stop trying to help God. You, yourself, must exercise self-control and quiet your own heart before God. Even God will give you the grace to do this. Then, be *still, stand in awe, wait* and *see*--be expectant for God's answers.

When David wrote Psalm 23, he knew what it was like to lie down beside the quiet waters of rest. God had taught him how to rest. God Himself led him to where his soul was restored and where he could walk in peace. Oh, will we let God lead us there through trust and prayer? A place where we hear only God. Where we are aware of the moment only—not borrowing from all our tomorrows.

Dear Father, place your hand upon our minds and quiet our rushing anxious thoughts. Place your hand on our hearts and still the turmoil and the churning waves.

I like the way the NLT translates verse 7. "Be still in the presence of the Lord."

Now, what else are we to do? What works hand in hand with resting in God? Waiting for God. The NLT says "…and wait patiently for Him to act." This word *wait* is fascinating to me because it is so difficult to do, and God asks us to do just that. He wouldn't ask us to do something we couldn't do. But first, again, let us get some Hebrew flavor on the word "wait." There is a double meaning to *wait*. On one hand, it means resting and on the other it means travailing (2342). When God asks us to rest and to be still before Him, there is still something active going on. It is a mystery. In our waiting, we are like a pregnant woman about to give birth. We have labor pains. As we do, we are to press into God trusting more fully, praising and adoring Him. We are to be in prayer and doing those things that God has shown us to do.

We are uncomfortable in our pain, yet we must wait. Something is taking shape around us, and in us. God is performing a work we cannot touch. We can only wait and praise Him for it, asking Him to deliver in His time. We tarry, we tremble, and we trust, we wait. Our patience is stretched and tested. God is performing a miracle of character in us at the same time He's answering our petitions.

Oh God, we are pregnant with expectancy to see You move on our behalf. Oh God deliver us and be glorified!

Pregnant with hope! We are to stay steady holding on to our hope, allowing God's inner working to take place inside us. Resting and waiting go hand in hand. The doctor tells the pregnant woman to go home and rest. How can she rest? But, she tries and in resting she is waiting, doing those things she knows are good for herself and the baby inside her. She cannot hurry the process, nor shape the child in her womb, but she is hopefully expecting something good! Something good

Hope In A Season Of Suffering

is coming to you, Dear One, as you struggle to trust, rest, and wait upon your God who loves you.

We must not try to hurry Him, for He is God and does all things well—right in His time. There is a purposed time for each matter under heaven, so we are to hold steady before God. We are to keep going about our lives as usual unless He shows us something more we can do about the matter. Then we must trust, rest, and wait again.

Remember: The acid test of how strong our faith is, at the time, is how much we are resting in God, waiting for His next move. God will always show us what to do, where to go, whom to talk to as we depend upon Him.

Discussion Questions:

1. What do we try to do in times of suffering?
2. When we have done all we can then what must we do?
3. How many times do we have to let go of something and trust God?
4. What does God do when we give Him our burdens?

Bible Study:

1. Turn to the book of Lamentations in the Old Testament. In Lamentations 3:25-26 to whom is the Lord good? In verse 25, what does it mean to be "good" to someone? In verse 26,

what do you think God means when He says to hope and wait "quietly"?

2. Psalm 37:3- 8, 27, and 34. Label what we are to do in order of appearance.

3. What are we to do when we can't make sense of the suffering that's going on in our lives, or around us? Proverbs 3:5-6.

4. Let us close with Matthew 11:28-29 and Psalm 23:1-2. According to Matthew, when we come to Jesus with our burdens what can we depend upon Him to give us?

5. What does "rest" mean to you?

6. And Psalm 23, because Jesus is our Good Shepherd and takes care of all our needs we can depend upon Him. What will He show us to do in verse 2?

7. What are some ways that He has done this in your own life?

Summary of Truths

Now let us run through the seven ways we can have more perseverance and steady hope while we are going through our sufferings.

1. Know God Personally.
2. Develop A Right Mindset.
3. Have Encouraging Hand-holders.
4. Pray Always in Everything.
5. Let God Develop and Use You.
6. Get Away with God.
7. Let God Work While You Trust, Rest, and Wait.

<u>Suffering is helpful when:</u>

- We turn to God for understanding, endurance, and deliverance.
- We ask important questions we might not take time to think about in our normal routine.
- It prepares us to identify with and comfort others who suffer.
- We are open to being helped by others who are obeying God.
- We are ready to learn from a trustworthy God.
- We realize we can identify with what Christ suffered on the cross for us.
- We are sensitized to the amount of suffering in the world.

<u>Suffering is harmful when:</u>

- We become hardened and reject God.
- We refuse to ask any questions and miss any lessons that might be good for us.
- We allow it to make us self-centered and selfish.
- We withdraw from the help others can give.
- We reject the fact that God can bring good out of calamity.
- We accuse God of being unjust and perhaps lead others to reject Him.
- We refuse to be open to any changes in our lives.

--Anonymous

Chapter 7
God's Personal Plan for You

More thoughts on Hope in a Season of Suffering

This section of the book presents more lessons on suffering and holding on to hope.

God's plan for us always includes salvation, that is, having us come to know Him, having our sins forgiven, receiving eternal life, and being placed into the family of God. God's plan for us also includes *suffering*, *restoration* and *serving*, then living forever in heaven with Him. This chapter will be on the part of God's plan that includes: **Suffering, Restoration and Serving.** (My emphasis will be on suffering and restoration.)

Through my own suffering state, God had brought me to Himself. He began to use my excruciating state of panic, terrifying fears, along with phobias and sinking depression, the total imbalance in my brain chemistry because of the break down I experienced at seventeen, to slowly bring about my healing, restoration, and preparation for His future plans and service for me. I was in the process of being restored. This was, and is, in itself, a process that is continual as we go from strength to strength. But, God does not wait until we are all healed up and perfectly whole to place us in His service –we learn to live the words of the Bible, "When I am weak then I am strong" (2 Corinthians 12:10).

Through my years of walking with Jesus, I have come to see this pattern of *suffering, restoration, and serving*, as consistent in my life, but I couldn't believe how much suffering I had endured. Over the past years, I have come to view suffering as a vital tool in our lives for bringing about great benefit and great good. Suffering bears good things if we let it. Now let's look at why suffering is included in God's personal plan for our lives.

The Necessity of Suffering

Suffering beautifies our spirit by developing character in us.

We desperately need godly character, as I mentioned earlier in the section on some of the reasons why we go through trials. When we allow suffering to make us humble, giving us a meek and gentle spirit, this is honorable before God. The harder the trial, the sharper the cutting tools, the meeker we are to become. Instead of accusing, blaming, being filled with anger, bitterness, and resentment, we need to learn to put things into perspective and to choose the attitudes that will please God. What happens inside of our hearts and minds during the suffering process is a mystery. However, I do know that **suffering + humility + obedience + time = Growth, healing, and restoration.**

We can learn from the analogy of silver being purified by the silversmith. When silver is being refined, it needs to be held in the center of the fire where the hottest temperature is, so that the impurities are burned away. But, the silver cannot be left there all by itself in the center; the silversmith must always have his eyes watching it every moment because if the silver is left a minute too long in the flame it will become unusable. It is only when the silversmith can see his own image on the face of the silver that he knows it is ready to be taken out of the fire. So, in Malachi 3:3, you can be assured that God, who is the great Refiner, who is sitting over the fires purifying your life, knows exactly when to pull you out, and He will not wait a moment longer or shorter.

Suffering causes our hearts to be more pliable and willing to obey.

Suffering teaches us obedience and makes us more *willing* to obey God. As we allow suffering to humble us and allow God's hands to mold us, we become more pliable. It is harder for us if we fight against God and resist His hand working in us. We all know what this is like, don't we? Choosing to obey God means choosing to obey His Word as opposed to practicing sin, following our sinful nature, which wants to wallow in self-pity, wants to blame and stay spiritually and emotionally crippled. Through suffering, God gets our hearts in the place He has desired, and then true restoration can begin.

Suffering causes us to depend on God for daily grace, strength, and provisions and not on ourselves.

As we are in the process of suffering, feeling so very uncomfortable and weak, we become painfully aware of our tremendous need for help from someone greater, and stronger than ourselves. The Bible declares that God, Himself, is that One. We must depend upon Him for the daily things we need in life, whether food, shelter, clothing, health, direction, strength, peace of mind, emotional stability, or guidance.

Remember, the very things we are weak in and suffer with are the very things that God uses to make us strong. Our own little thread of hope and strength is attached and solidified into His eternally strong unbreakable rope of mighty strength and power. Thus, He carries us across to the other side of suffering which is peace and joy, bearing the fruit of goodness, stability and of course, hope. And truly, again, what happens inside of us is a mystery when out of our weaknesses we are made strong in His strength.

Suffering strengthens, establishes, and settles us deeper in our most precious faith, though tried by fire.

As a muscle is made strong by exerting it against a heavier force, so is our faith made strong through the heavy weights of the things which we suffer. As we *choose* to trust in Christ and depend on Him, we begin to rest more and experience increased inner stability of faith.

Suffering includes waiting periods so God can accomplish His goals for us, in us and through us.

I spoke of "waiting" in an earlier chapter; it is extremely hard to wait on God and wait on His timing concerning things to be accomplished in our lives and around us. We are tempted to take things into our own hands and jump ahead of God. Waiting is one of the most important lessons we can learn; I am always learning to wait--until God moves in a situation, until I hear God speak, until He has accomplished all His will in me. Waiting takes patience and it is very frustrating at times. God, however, is not in a rush or hurry with our lives.

The Beauty of Restoration

God gave me a promise that He, Himself, would restore to my life what the locusts had eaten, all the years that seemed endless with suffering. God began to bring people, books, music, and other agents into my life to bring about my healing and wholeness. Different pieces of the puzzle that seemed to be missing were slowly being uncovered and began to fit into place. Slowly, faith began to replace fear, and joyful expectation began to replace the dark depression.

I have experienced so much freedom and my heart overflows with thanksgiving to the Lord who does all things well. The Bible tells us in Ecclesiastes 3:11 that "He has made everything beautiful in its time." There is a particular time that God has for us to become beautiful in an area that we have been struggling with. We must also not forget that healing is a journey and continual process.

God is in the business of not only allowing us to be torn down, but also building us up and restoring us. Again, in Ecclesiastes 3:3 we are told that there is a "time to tear down and a time to build." God builds on a good foundation, so we may find ourselves stripped down to bare roots in an area of our lives. God builds what He desires in us so that we can serve Him fully, be filled with joy, and bring Him glory. As a new creation in Christ, our spirit has been made brand new, but our mind needs to be transformed. This is part of the restoring process. I have found restoration has three main ingredients: 1) *The Working of the Holy Spirit, 2) Knowing and Obeying God's Word, the Bible, and 3) the Passing of Time.*

1) *The Working of the Holy Spirit.*

In order for true healing to be active in our lives, the Holy Spirit of God must be at work in us. It is God who works with us in the process of restoration. God is constantly at work transforming our hearts (emotions, will, and attitudes) and our minds (intellect and processor of information). To be healed we need to cultivate a new attitude, a new vision, renewed hope, greater humility, and submissiveness. Plus, we must believe God's Word that He is the Healer and that He does heal today. It is the Holy Spirit that takes our efforts and combines them with His power to bring about change in our lives. Therefore, it is vital that we are sensitive to His leading. It is also the Holy Spirit who guides us and opens our eyes to glimpses of hope when we are in the clouds of depression and feel hopeless. It is crucial to hold on to these glimpses of hope and reality when they come—they are our silver lining in the dark cloud.

2) *Knowing and Obeying God's Word, the Bible*

What is required of us in working out our salvation, and our healing? It is our responsibility to get to know what God's Word says, about God Himself, about our own hearts, the renewing of our minds, and obedience in our situation. Through Bible studies on our own or in a group, we grow to know God's Word. We need to know what God says about things. Once we know, then we can obey, and with obeying comes empowerment through the Holy Spirit. Thus, will come redirection and restoration of that which has been broken down.

Our daily time in God's Word is extremely important for us to hear His guidance for our situation and lives. As we step forward in obedience, to forgive rather than to hold a grudge, to praise rather than pout, to give rather than withhold, to love rather than hate…God brings into our lives just the healing instruments we need for our hearts to mend. He uses His Word, His presence, strategic people, directed books, certain situations, our children, our families, even our pets, and nature itself to restore our health.

3) Time

We need the passing of time for healing to be accomplished in us. There will be break-throughs in areas where we have been wrestling--we will find peace instead of turmoil. We need to allow ourselves much time to be restored and to heal. If we don't, we may find ourselves growing angry, frustrated, still grieving, becoming bitter and resentful. Remember that God is in no hurry.

Allow yourself to be forgiven, helped, comforted, and encouraged. Don't shove love away from you when it presents itself. Take the hand of that person who wants to make amends; and when genuine godly love offers itself, embrace it, be loved. And be made whole.

Wonderful Service

God uses us as we work with Him, in all the stages of our lives, whether broken or mended, laughing or crying, full or empty. We have just what we need to give and to help when God positions us in ministry. Remember that ministry is where God has put you right now. But, there is also a bigger and greater destination of where God is leading us. He wants us to fulfill and do His works so that others may see, hear, and believe in Him. So, in whatever capacity God calls you to serve Him, do it with all your heart; this is God's plan for you. It will bring you joy as well as satisfaction as you invest in eternal things. Amen.

ROXANNE EILERS

"For I know the plans I have for you," says the Lord. "They are plans for good and not for disaster, to give you a future and a hope" (Jeremiah 29:11).

I would like to state here that it is vitally important to continue to seek out those sources that will be of comfort, support and encouragement to you in your painful season. I have mentioned different sources throughout my book that I believe will be of great benefit to you. A last source I'd like to add is for grieving a loss. Barbara LesStrang Baumann is a grief coach and wrote the book, *After-Loss: A Recovery Companion for Those Who Are Grieving*; it is a powerful companion to have in time of need.

Chapter 8
Encouraging Quotes

"Never does a man know the force that is in him till some mighty affliction or grief has humanized the soul." Author: Frederick W. Robertson

"No character is ultimately tested until it has suffered." Author: Harry Emerson Fosdick

"All the world is full of suffering. It is also full of overcoming." Author: Helen Keller

"Character cannot be developed in ease and quiet. Only through experience of trial and suffering can the soul be strengthened, ambition inspired, and success achieved." Author: Helen Keller

"Hope is not the absence of grief, sorrow, fear or worry. Hope is knowing that you are not alone in your experience and that you will have the strength to make it through." Author: Roxanne Eilers

"Let God enlarge you when you are going through distress. He can do it. You can't do it, and others can't do it for you." Author: Warren Wiersbe

"At the timberline where the storms strike with the most fury, the sturdiest trees are found." Author: Hudson Taylor

"Snuggle in God's arms. When you are hurting, when you feel lonely, left out. let Him cradle you, comfort you, reassure you of His all-sufficient power and love." Author: Kay Arthur

"The readiest way to escape from our sufferings is, to be willing they should endure as long as God pleases." Author: John Wesley

"God will not permit any troubles to come upon us, unless He has a specific plan by which great blessing can come out of the difficulty." Author: Peter Marshall

"Let us not be surprised when we have to face difficulties. When the wind blows hard on a tree, the roots stretch and grow the stronger; let it be so with us. Let us not be weaklings, yielding to every wind that blows, but strong in spirit to resist." Author: Amy Carmichael

"It takes but one positive thought when given a chance to survive and thrive to overpower an entire army of negative thoughts." Author: Robert H. Schuller

"It is the crushed grape that yields the wine."
- *Author Unknown*

"God uses the suffering that we experience to make us more like Jesus. He is not the cause of the suffering, rather He is the healer—He is the remedy." Author: Roxanne Eilers

"You need not cry very loud, He is nearer to us than we think." Author: Brother Lawrence

"Heartache forces us to embrace God out of desperate urgent need. God is never closer than when your heart is aching." Author: Joni Eareckson Tada

"Our sorrows are all, like ourselves, mortal. There are no immortal sorrows for immortal souls. They come, but blessed be God, they also go. Like birds of the air they fly over our heads. But they cannot make their abode in our souls. We suffer today, but we shall rejoice tomorrow." Author: Charles Spurgeon

"Our vision is so limited we can hardly imagine a love that does not show itself in protection from suffering.... The love of God did not protect His Own Son.... He will not necessarily protect us - not from anything it takes to make us like His Son. A lot of hammering and chiseling and purifying by fire will have to go into the process." Author: Elisabeth Elliot

"Grace grows best in winter." Author: Samuel Rutherford

"Can a mother forget the baby at her breast and have no compassion on the child she has borne? Though she may forget, I will not forget you! See, I have engraved you on the palms of my hands; your walls are ever before me (Isaiah 49:15-16)." Author: God

"....joy runs deeper than despair." Author: Corrie Ten Boom

"The remedy for discouragement is the Word of God. When you feed your heart and mind with its truth, you regain your perspective and find renewed strength." Author: Warren Wiersbe

"Christian, remember the goodness of God in the frost of adversity." Author: Charles Spurgeon

"Trials teach us what we are; they dig up the soil, and let us see what we are made of." Author: Charles Spurgeon

"Adversity is not simply a tool. It is God's most effective tool for the advancement of our spiritual lives. The circumstances and events that we see as setbacks are oftentimes the very things that launch us into periods of intense spiritual growth. Once we begin to understand this, and accept it as a spiritual fact of life, adversity becomes easier to bear." Author: Charles Stanley

"Adversity is always unexpected and unwelcomed. It is an intruder and a thief, and yet in the hands of God, adversity becomes the means through which His supernatural power is demonstrated." Author: Charles Stanley

"I realize anew that, just as we must learn to obey God one choice at a time, we must also learn to trust God one circumstance at a time. Trusting God is not a matter of my feelings but of my will. I never feel like trusting God when adversity strikes, but I can choose to do so even when I don't feel like it. That act of the will, though, must be based on belief, and belief must be based on truth." Author: Jerry Bridges

Chapter 9
Epilogue I, Before

Today is a new day, and God is at work in my life. Just today, I was in a situation where I was lost in traffic. I was in an area that I didn't know, and the more I drove around, the more lost I became. I began to panic and feel helpless, very small. Then I thought to myself, what am I saying to myself? I was telling myself that it was terrible being lost, and that I would just lose it—panic and have to have someone come and pick me up—rescue me. Then, I told myself the truth. I'm lost all right but I can always ask at a gas station for directions (No, I don't have a navigator. Perhaps I should get one!). I can also call the police and ask them for help. Eventually, I will come to a street that is familiar. I don't need to panic; I can take care of myself—I will get to where I am going safely with God's help. And I did.

My struggles are never over, but I have learned tools that can help me through them. Many of these tools I have shared with you in this book. I am no longer living in a world of depression and unreality, and I choose to face whatever I have to go through instead of shrinking from it. I know that it will probably always be a growing process when I travel— new places, new faces. I'm constantly being stretched to come out of my safe little cocoon. I get comfortable with what I am doing and where I am, and then the Lord brings a challenging change into my life. Life would be boring if things didn't ever change. I don't want to be boring so I must change in areas where I need to.

Don't ever think that you are alone in your suffering. I am with you, God is with you; there are many, many others who are with you. Don't be afraid to face your fears, one fear at a time. Don't be afraid to feel pain and discomfort; don't be afraid to feel and receive love, joy, and peace either. I remember how hard it was for me to feel love. Over time, I learned to let love into my heart and to really receive it, especially from the Lord Jesus. I also recall that I couldn't feel joy because of my sore afflicted emotions. Every time something good would happen, I wouldn't allow myself to enjoy it, but I would find something that would quickly snatch away my joy. But now I have overcome this--I can feel joy! I love it! And peace—I never had peace; that was something I could only dream of and hope I would experience some day. Well, today I am much more at peace with God, myself, others, and the world. I don't fuss about the little things; I don't get myself all riled up over a matter. If my husband shrinks a new beautiful blouse of mine, I say, "Oh well, it was nice when I bought it, but it is just a material thing. Shrinking does happen-- mistakes when washing do happen, but it's not terrible." And then I move on to the next thing.

Life is too short to be angry all the time, blaming others, criticizing others, or complaining all the time. I want to enjoy life to its fullest! Jesus said, "I am come to give you life and that abundantly!" I want this kind of life and so I will continue seeking God, loving Him and others, working to do what is good in

ROXANNE EILERS

His sight, and blessing others. I will enjoy smelling the fragrance of roses in my neighbor's yard as I go for a walk; I will bend down and breathe in the perfume of the jasmine vine. I will take delight in the little things in life, like going shopping, stopping to visit my mother who is ninety-three, reading a book, riding bikes with my husband, talking with my son, eating a chocolate brownie, going to lunch with a balcony person; and I could go on and on.

I suppose I will be living new chapters all the time throughout my journey. Thank you so much for being part of these chapters in this book by reading them. Much encouragement to you in your journey; and much blessing and comfort to you.

Chapter 10
Epilogue II, Today

Some years have passed since I first wrote this book. God has waited for the time of its publication. This is just a short catch up on my life and what I am doing.

Recently, my husband and I just lost our only son, Joseph, in a car accident. He was only 22 and still at home with us. He went to heaven on February 15, 2016. My life has now been turned upside down and I have had to hold steadfastly to all that I ever and always believed in. I have experienced such grief and sorrow that I never knew before now. I have had to keep my eyes heaven bound to keep afloat during these months. My relationship with my heavenly Father has deepened as I have run to Him for comfort and hope. He is the God of all comfort and hope. Everything that I have shared in this book about how to keep your hope alive in a time of suffering has once again been tested, and yes, it works if we do it.

Remember the seven concepts:

1. Know God Personally.
2. Develop a Right Mindset.
3. Have Encouraging Hand-Holders.
4. Pray Always in Everything.
5. Let God Use You and Your Gifts.
6. Get Away With God.
7. Let God Work While You Trust, Rest and Wait.

Thank God I have chosen to *know Him personally* through His Son, Jesus Christ. I have purposed to grow in my relationship with Him over the years. Then, I have had to examine what I was saying to myself about what happened to my son, my changed situation, my emotions of grief. My *mindset* has been greatly challenged during this time, and I have set my thoughts on God's Word to bring transformation to any wrong thinking and have told myself the truth about my situation. One truth that combats discouragement and despair is that *I always have hope and a purpose given to me by God.*

Again, I have chosen to gravitate to those who are *encouraging hand-holders*--those who will support and build me up and tell me the truth. They help me get a better perspective of my situation and life when I find myself in a hole of darkness and gloom. God's people have been huge instruments in helping me heal from this time of grief. How they love me as I am.

Yes, I have had to *pray always* and keep my heart focused on the Savior's love and grace for me. Prayer, for me, is a must—no questions asked, no arguments. When I stay connected with God I can stand anything that comes my way—even the death of my only son.

I have watched the Father bring me out of the depths of despair through the *use of the gifts* He has blessed me with. I choose to give of myself when I can, and this has brought tremendous healing. My main purpose on this earth is to glorify God and serve

Him. This includes doing the things He asks me to do even when I don't feel like it.

Getting away with God is what I do every day. I am gobbling up books on spiritual growth and healing from grief. I am getting to know my Lord more intimately and I am finding my focus is becoming clearer and clearer as I spend time in His presence. I listen to Him speak to me through His Word, the Holy Spirit and through all the ways He knows He can reach me.

Finally, I am realizing I cannot always control things that happen in my life, but I can choose to *let God work* good out of what has the potential to ruin me. I am always learning to lean upon Him for my needs and to cease my striving and struggling to manage the situation (which I can't manage anyway). I am learning to just be with Him and be me. Then, of course, I will always be waiting for something good to happen—something good in the future, where God is taking me on this journey.

Dear Father, please continue to make me more like Jesus. Use my life to touch another's. Let me make a difference in my world for the time I am here. Keep me seeking things above and be that person who does that one thing that will bless others.

I know that God is at work in you today as well, and I am excited about what He is making of your life. Remember this, my friend, always, always be hopeful—always hold on to those glimpses of hope that pop in your mind during a difficult time. That is

God, infusing hope into your valley. Keep holding on to hope in spite of circumstances and situations—God will see you through. I also want to invite you to write to me sharing your thoughts and comments or simply email me. I'd love to hear from you. Remember I believe in you and care about your journey too. God bless you richly!

"You turned my wailing into dancing; You removed my sackcloth and clothed me with joy, that my heart may sing Your praises and not be silent. Lord my God, I will praise You forever" (Psalm 30:11-12).

To contact me, my address is:
Eilers Ministries, Inc.,
P.O. Box 10783,
Palm Desert, CA. 92255.
My email is: Roxanne@EilersMin.com.

For speaking engagements, please contact the above address, or call 760-396-6110.

End Notes

Aschenbrenner, George A. "Consciousness Examen." Jesuit Center for Spiritual Growth, 1993.

Backus, William and Marie Chapian. *Telling Yourself the Truth*. Minneapolis, Minnesota: Bethany House, 1980.

Baumann, Barbara LesStrang. *After-Loss: A Recovery Companion for Those Who Are Grieving*. Nashville: Thomas Nelson, Inc., 1992. Griefcoach@aol.com

Brandt, Robert L. *Spiritual Gifts*. Brussels, Belgium: International Correspondence Institute, 1978.

Bridges, Jerry. *Trusting God Even When Life Hurts*. Colorado Springs, Colorado:Navpress, 1988.

Cornwall, Judson. *Praying the Scriptures*. Florida: Creation House, 1990.

Fortune, Don & Katie. *Discover Your God-Given Gifts*. Grand Rapids, Michigan: Chosen Books, 1987.

Getz, Gene A. *Building Up One Another*. La Habra, California: The Lockman Foundation, 1972.

Heatherly, Joyce Landorf. *Balcony People*. Georgetown, Texas: Balcony Publishing Inc.,1989.

Heuser, Roger and Norman Shawchuck. *Leading the Congregation: Caring for Yourself While Serving Others*. Nashville: Abingdon Press, 2010.

Keating, Thomas. *Intimacy With God: Centering Prayer*. New York: Crossroad Publishing, 2012.

Martin, Catherine. "Quiet Time Ministries." P.O. Box 14007, Palm Desert, Ca. 92255; 760-772-2357 www.quiettime.org

Murray, Andrew. *The Master's Indwelling*. United States: Whitaker House, 1983.

Murray, Andrew. "Within Or the Kingdom of God is Within You." Service and Paton,1897. From the Mowbray Convention revised for publication, 1996.

Nouwen, Henri. *In the Name of Jesus*. New York: The Crossroad Publishing Co., 1989.

Payne, Leanne. *The Healing Presence*. Wheaton, Illinois: Crossway Books, 1989.

Packer, J.I. *Knowing God*. London: Hodder and Stoughton, 1973.

Ray, David. *The Art of Christian Meditation.* Wheaton, Illinois: Tyndale House, 1977.

Schwartz, Jeffrey M. *Brain Lock*. New York: Regan Books, 1996.

Smith, Hannah Whitall. *The Christian's Secret of a Happy Life*. Christian Witness Co.,1875.

Smith, Hannah Whitall. *The God of All Comfort*. Chicago: Moody Press, 1956.

Yancey, Philip. *Where is God When It Hurts?* Grand Rapids, Michigan: Zondervan, 1977.